THE BULLY BLOCKER

THE **BULLY BLOCKER**
A play and other resources

**ANNEKA CHAMPION
and EVELYN M. FIELD**

amba
press

Published by Amba Press
Melbourne, Australia
www.ambapress.com.au

Editor: Sarah Fallon
Cover designer : Tess McCabe

Printed by IngramSpark

ISBN: 9781923215467 (pbk)
ISBN: 9781923215474 (ebk)

A catalogue record for this book is available from the National Library of Australia.

CONTENTS

INTRODUCTION
BY ANNEKA

Teaching is a demanding profession and many of you are time poor already. On top of this, bullying behaviours are on the rise.

The antics of bullies and the injuries inflicted on their targets disrupt your classroom and play havoc with the civility of the school yard. Yet another issue for teachers to manage. Another energy drainer to pull focus from the job of getting through an already crowded curriculum.

Reducing levels of bullying in schools would be life-changing for society but the challenge of that is complex. While waiting (impatiently) for policies and social changes to stem the rise of bullying, what can you do to help your students manage their response to bullying?

The materials in this book aim to help you with that challenge.

Another, equally important, goal of this book is to help your students learn about the damaging, sometimes tragic, consequences for an individual who is bullied. This awareness raising may lead to stopping or reducing some bullying behaviours. It may resonate sufficiently for some students to give pause to how they treat others. That would be a wonderful outcome.

Human beings are all too human

Realistically, even with a deeper understanding of the harms of bullying, some students will continue to bully others. Possibly they witness bullying at home, or as part of the broader school culture, or on the sports field, and repeat those negative behaviours. Perhaps they're just insensitive, have underdeveloped emotional intelligence or have not had the benefit of positive role models in their lives.

The stark fact is that statistically some of your students will be suffering from being bullied, some will be bullies and many others will be bystanders to the problem – complicit perhaps by their silence or actively participating because peer pressure to join in feels less confronting than the risk of being humiliated and ostracised themselves. There are no winners when bullying is not addressed and managed effectively.

Regardless of whether any one of your students fall into the category of being a bully, a target or a bystander – and they may even assume all three roles in different contexts – the primary focus of this resource is to arm *all* students with a tool kit to handle being bullied.

Even those who are the obvious bullies in your classroom may one day find themselves on the other end of the stick. We all deserve to learn the valuable life skill of managing our response to bullying.

Evidence; not wishful thinking

This book, firmly grounded in the evidence-based work of Evelyn M. Field, psychologist, offers a structure to teach these skills to your students in a fun and engaging way.

I have summarized the key elements of Evelyn's work into:

1. A relatable story line in the play script *The Bully Blocker*
2. Accompanying user-friendly teaching resources

Benefits of a playscript

Using a playscript is a playful resource for teachers. By its very structure, a play and its characters, gives your students freedom to play, explore, reflect, practice and learn.

The Bully Blocker allows the emotive topic of bullying to be explored in a safe, inclusive and reflective way. By focusing on the script and its characters, it reduces pressure on students. It provides space between any emotional reactions they have to the topic, and a frank discussion and exploration of the issues. Just as the characters in the play make discoveries and evolve, your students too can go on a journey where they become empowered by the skills they learn and practice.

The Bully Blocker gives an opportunity for all students – but especially for less confident ones – to explore this topic through the safety of assuming a character. Most of the roles are 'dogs' (albeit dogs with the ability to walk on two legs and the power of speech along with human-like personalities and very human problems). This device permits even greater emotional space between students acting the roles and the issues being probed.

Getting yourself up to speed

Many of us grew up hearing conflicting advice about how to handle being bullied – fight back, ignore it or tell the bully to stop. Evidence shows that none of these approaches help the bullied child.

Until I became aware of Evelyn's work, I thought that *'ignore it'* was the best way to respond and years ago offered this advice to my own children. Like me, when I first encountered Evelyn's work, many of you may be on a steep learning curve.

There are seven scenes in the script with each scene exploring several concepts aimed at building:

- your class's understanding of the impacts of bullying
- evidence-based skills which help a student cope effectively if they get bullied

There is a corresponding chapter of supporting materials based on each scene with content on the key concepts, discussion prompts and a range of activities related to the topics raised. The resources for Scenes Three and Five are significantly longer than the others and could fill two lessons each; meaning the overall material can facilitate nine lessons.

How you use the materials will naturally depend on your judgment for the age group, school culture and any current problems within the cohort you are teaching.

The key concepts can be 'taught' by you if you decide that best suits your class needs.

Or you may decide after a read through of each scene to dive straight into discussion and activities. Again, which discussion prompts and activities you choose will depend on age group, time available and educational needs.

Each chapter has working materials for the corresponding scene under the following headings:

- Cast members in the scene
- Props required
- Precis
- Concepts: key theory
- A range of discussion prompts and activities

Basics of the script

The Bully Blocker features thirteen characters with an active role.

There is also the Wise Chorus in each scene.

For less confident students, a role in the chorus gives them the opportunity to have a speaking role within the safety of a group. There are suggested lines for different chorus members but these are a guide only – the chorus lines can be allocated to as few, or as many, students as works in your circumstances.

The chorus is written in an easy-to-follow rhythm of 8/6/8/6 and with a consistent rhyme scheme of A/B/C/B. This structure should facilitate easy participation.

For those students who are unable or unwilling to take on a reading/speaking role, each scene ends with 'music makers' creating a soundscape to reflect the mood of the scene. The 'instruments' used to create the soundscape can be sophisticated (if you have access to actual instruments like tambourines, clapping sticks, recorders) or as basic as hand clapping and vocal sounds.

You could also appoint a 'stage manager' to handle the props or a Wise Chorus manager to conduct the lines. The aim is to create the opportunity for involvement of all students irrespective of their confidence and the resources available to you.

Perhaps your class or school's drama department may be inspired to perform the play before an audience ...

However you make use of it, I sincerely hope *The Bully Blocker* script and related activities prove to be educationally useful as well as heaps of fun for you and your class.

So, on with the play!

Best wishes

Anneka Champion

INTRODUCTION
BY EVELYN

The Bully Blocking story

During the severe Melbourne COVID-19 pandemic lockdown, I was inspired by my little dog Harry, to write *Harry the Bully Blocker* with Sean Doyle. This wonderful little book is bully blocking therapy in a nutshell, both for kids and adults. We later decided to release it as an audiobook and this is how we met Anneka, who narrated it.

Around that time, I attended an event at the home of Hyonju Neeman, a Board Member of the Melbourne Symphony Orchestra. I listened as a few other guests, members of the MSO, discussed their school's program, which encourages students to experience fun and interactive workshops while engaging with orchestral music and instruments.

This sparked a new idea. I discussed with Sean the idea of turning *Harry the Bully Blocker* into a play which involves every student in the class, so that they can actively experience the bully blocking message. Soon after, I began updating my school bullying book and in 2024, *Bully Blocking: Empowering students to manage bullying* was released.

Sean mentioned the idea of a play to Anneka Champion, and she loved it! Thus, Anneka has used her own experience and insights together with *Harry the Bully Blocker* (2021) and *Bully Blocking: Empowering students to manage bullying* (2024) to create a play which I hope will empower each child to experience the thrill of becoming a real bully blocker!

Bullying can be traumatic!

Around the world, one in three children are bullied at school. Some students block the bullying behaviours and earn the respect of peers, others lack strategies, become submissive or feel powerless, helpless and paralysed. They arrive at school filled with fear, frustration and helplessness, knowing they may be bullied again. The constant fear of being bullied, makes them feel even more defenceless, ashamed and isolated. Weak friends abandon them, and gutless friends betray them.

Some kids feel too ashamed to ask for advice and support. Others try ineffectual advice from well-meaning adults like *'Do nothing, walk away, tell the bully to stop.'* Clinical practice shows this doesn't work and often leads to the child feeling worse, especially when the advice from trusted adults fails.

Bullied kids regard school as a traumatic and painful experience. Understandably many will resist or refuse to attend school. These children realise that many teachers can't stop the bullying. They don't tell their parents because they don't want to upset them, they sense their powerlessness or fear they may make the bullying worse. They feel shame, embarrassment and guilt and bear this burden alone. Many only tell adults when they are at breaking point, though without expectation that adults can help long-term.

Some bullied children see the only solution to their trauma is to harm themselves or others. They retreat into their own world, suffering personal, physical, academic and social losses.

Sadly, while many adults regard school bullying as a harmless rite of passage, the current evidence nullifies this belief. Bullying interferes with a student's normal progression through the main physical, psychological, cognitive and social developmental stages of childhood and adolescence. Bullying represents humiliation ('You're no good') and ostracism ('You're not wanted, get out'). Children feel excluded from their tribe and this threatens their social survival. Thus, bullying attacks the social connectivity areas of the human brain. The brain switches into survival mode and releases toxic stress hormones. If this continues over a long period of time the level of those hormones becomes toxic and can injure the brain forever. A sobering fact!

The role of society, the school and family

Recent research (Rigby 2021) indicates that four out of five school bullying programs don't actually work. They may be solid in theory, research and even practice, but don't work because:

- Schools don't take the neurological damage caused by bullying seriously
- Schools don't consistently apply preventative programs, evidence-based interventions and suitable consequences across the whole school
- Schools don't audit and rectify unsuccessful school bullying programs
- Parents aren't involved, coached and supported when bullying occurs
- Schools fail to teach effective bully blocking strategies to students
- Schools don't reduce workplace bullying among teachers, senior management and boards

The approach taken by most schools reflects our broader society by adopting an adversarial approach to solving disputes. Someone wins; someone loses. Instead, bullying needs to be regarded as a symptom of systemic dysfunction – a relationship breakdown that requires respectful, collaborative and restorative solutions i.e. a win/win outcome.

However, we can help you teach students effective bully blocking skills to equip them to manage their responses and reduce the harm done to them. We can also support parents in creating positive, constructive, non-abusive homes where children are treated with respect and enabled to grow in socially, healthy ways without being cut off at their psycho-social roots like a bonsai.

Why does bullying occur?

Bullying occurs within a context of intertwining systems – including the state system, local laws and culture, the school and the family system. Bullying is most common between children aged 8 to 16 which aligns with the child's search for an individual and a social identity.

Bullying is a game where some students systematically abuse their power. The game may continue over years with the same players, or bullies may seek new targets. Some students are serial targets while some are serial bullies. Some switch roles depending on the situation. Some students move to schools and encounter bullying or social challenges again.

Bullies use the peer groups to maintain their power and status. When members of a peer group giggle out of fear, embarrassment or amusement when they witness bullying, they reward the bully. When students join in with the bully, they help strengthen the bully's power. The bully may behave well in class but exclude the target in the playground or socially. The bully may be a friend or someone within the target's social group. A group can invite a kid to join them, alienate them from decent friends and then reject them.

At an unconscious level, bullies want to embarrass their target to feel stronger and better. Consciously most bullies don't have a clue that they're bullying or that their behaviour is harmful. Few intend to injure the target and many are mortified and ashamed when outed as a bully. Regardless of their conscious or unconscious intent, bullies cause significant damage to the target, themselves and bystanders.

Sadly, we humans are often two-faced. We prize and despise bullies. We protect them with a conspiracy of silence and we're too ashamed to admit to our own bullying behaviours.

Bullying is anti-social and will always exist. However, our task as adult educators and carers is to support the children in our care and work out how to prevent, reduce and manage bullying appropriately.

The bully continuum

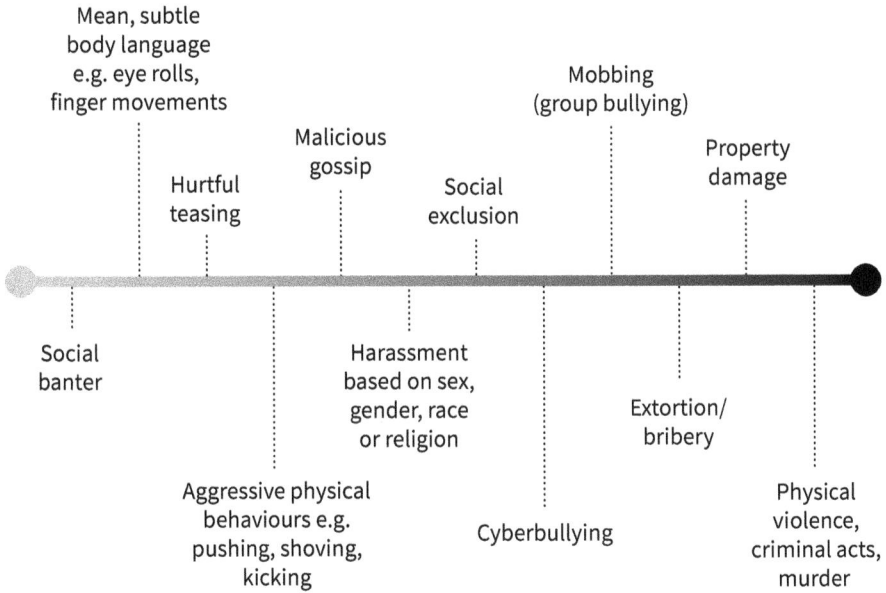

The bully continuum

Mean, subtle body language e.g. eye rolls, finger movements

Hurtful teasing

Malicious gossip

Social exclusion

Mobbing (group bullying)

Property damage

Social banter

Harassment based on sex, gender, race or religion

Extortion/ bribery

Aggressive physical behaviours e.g. pushing, shoving, kicking

Cyberbullying

Physical violence, criminal acts, murder

Empowering bully blockers and social beings!

School bullying presents as a 'doom and gloom' situation. Fortunately, the current evidence provides a range of behavioural options to help a student manage bullying and enjoy a normal social life.

Anyone who creates a good rapport with the bullied student can help them develop an understanding of their social survival instinct and coach them with simple, basic, natural bully blocking strategies. And increasingly, as there is greater awareness, academic research and informed clinical practice, we will see more effective antibullying policies, programs and resources.

If you're interested in further reading on the science and theory, you'll find more extensive material, research analysis and resources in the third edition of my book *Bully Blocking: Empowering students to manage bullying*.

Our task as adult educators is to support the children in our care and do our utmost to empower them to reduce and manage bullying at school, helping them to develop the skills that can also block bullying at home and, later, at work.

In this book, you have access to a playscript and supporting materials written by Anneka which encapsulate my evidence-based strategies for bully-blocking and demonstrates how they work experientially in practice. It's an extremely worthwhile and life-affirming resource!

Evelyn M. Field OAM, FAPS

THE BULLY BLOCKER
SCRIPT

Cast of characters

Wise Chorus 1–6:

- Each Wise Chorus role can be performed by one or more students depending on class size

Hair-parents (humans):

- Tilly
- Jake

Fur-babies:

- Chewy (a rescue dog of unknown mixed breed)
- Mimi (a French poodle)

Neighbourhood dogs:

- Sunny (a terrier cross)
- Mango (mixed breed)
- Petal (a pitbull)
- Hammer (a rottweiler)
- Diesel (a dobermann)
- Comrade (a labrador)
- Mellow (a retriever)
- Ziggy (a greyhound)

Mrs Shetland (aka Mrs S, a sheepdog), the school counsellor

Music makers: as many as class size allows

Props

These can be brought from home or handmade in class:

- Collars × 12 (two for Mimi including one which is sparkly and colourful, and one for each other dog character)
- Tails × 11 (optional – can be a piece of fabric or scarf tucked in or pinned to back)
- Leads × 2 (using a lead can be mimed if it feels safer)

- Dog bowls × 2
- Kibble – scrunched up brown paper pellets (optional – the kibble can be imagined)
- Dog poop bags
- A large stick
- Cool sunglasses
- E-phone (doesn't need to work or make one out of cardboard)
- Hairbrush

Note to performers

The dog characters can walk on two feet and speak English.

The human and dog characters understand each other.

Mimi uses some French words – the meanings are:

- *Je suis irresistible* – I am irresistible
- *Frere* – brother
- *Merde* – shit
- *Moi* – me

SCENE ONE

Wise Chorus 1 and 2 are onstage at stage left, where they can be seen clearly.

Tilly walks onstage from stage right with Chewy following on a lead. Jake follows with Mimi on a lead. Chewy is dragging his heels and looks miserable but Mimi bounces along confidently. Mimi has <u>attitude</u>.

TILLY	We're home now, Chewy. You can chill. That wasn't too bad, was it? You were a good dog.
MIMI	Seriously? He was a complete wuss.

Chewy glares at Mimi. Tilly removes Chewy's lead.

TILLY *(to Chewy)*	You had fun, didn't you?
MIMI *(sarcastic)*	If your definition of fun is not barking with anyone – sure, he had fun!
CHEWY	Shut up, Mimi! You don't know what it's like!

Jake removes Mimi's lead and follows it with a long pat on her back.

JAKE	And who's my lovely girl?
MIMI *(perky)*	That'd be *moi!* I'm your precious poodle.

It's the French in me. *Je suis irrésistible!*

TILLY *(to Jake)*   I worry about Chewy.
He's still not great socialising in a pack.

JAKE   Yeah, I know.
He really lets the other dogs get under
his fur.

WISE CHORUS 1   Chewy is an adopted dog,
A mixture of three breeds.

WISE CHORUS 2   He's sweet and kind and full of life
But has some complex needs.

Mimi struts around – confident and showy. She preens and brushes her tail. Jake makes a fuss of her.

JAKE   Good dog, good dog. Who's a good dog,
then?

Jake and Tilly walk offstage.

WISE CHORUS 1   Mimi is his older sister.
She's got a feisty face,
And a strong, magnificent tail –
She's da boss at their place.

Mimi bats her eyelashes extravagantly.

MIMI   What you up to now, Chewy?

CHEWY   Just chilling.

MIMI *(mimicking)*   Just chilling.
Don't let it wear you out.

CHEWY   Stop being mean!

Chewy slouches, timid and confused. He thinks aloud.

CHEWY *(continued)*   How would you like to be me?
I'm a sad excuse for a dog.
Useless, shy, I'm afraid of everything.
I'm utterly pathetic.

WISE CHORUS 2   The secret is in Chewy's mouth,
As he has dodgy teeth.
He knows his mouth is not quite right.
This gives him constant grief.

Tilly returns to the stage, bringing two dog bowls of kibble which she places downstage.

TILLY   Here you go.

MIMI   Yay, dinnertime!

TILLY *(to Mimi)*   Good dog. Yes, you are.

(to Chewy)   And you're a good dog, too.

Tilly walks offstage.
Chewy and Mimi eat the kibble – Chewy slowly and with difficulty. Mimi gulps her food.

WISE CHORUS 1   He has to eat quite carefully,
And Mimi takes his food.

Mimi pushes Chewy out of the way and eats from his bowl.

CHEWY *(pleading)*   Mimi, please don't ...

Mimi ignores him and keeps eating his food.

CHEWY   No, don't!

WISE CHORUS 1   This makes him hungry and angry
And in a grumpy mood.

Chewy wanders around miserably. Jake walks onstage with Sunny and Mango following him.

| JAKE | Hey guys, we've invited some of your friends over. |

Jake walks offstage while Sunny and Mango try to get Chewy to play.

| SUNNY | Hi Mimi, hi Chewy. Wanna play tag? |

| MIMI | Sure thing! |

Chewy shakes his head 'no'.

| MANGO | C'mon, I'll be 'it'. |

Chewy refuses to play.

| SUNNY | C'mon, please Chewy. It'll be fun! |

Chewy will not be cheered up.

| WISE CHORUS 2 | You know, some dogs do *like* Chewy
And come to him to play.
But he thinks they are just faking |

| WISE CHORUS 1 & 2 | And pushes them away! |

Chewy growls and barks at Mimi, Sunny and Mango.

| MIMI | Let's leave misery guts to himself. |

Mimi, Sunny and Mango run offstage.
Wise Chorus 3 and 4 walk onstage and stand in front of Wise Chorus 1 and 2. There's now a chorus of four students.

| WISE CHORUS 3 | Some dogs say nasty words to him
If Chewy comes too near
It's not that they dislike him, they
Just like to provoke fear! |

Petal and Hammer run onstage and circle Chewy menacingly.

| HAMMER | Do you appreciate how stupendously displeasing your mouth is? |

PETAL	Yeah, your mouth is crazy weird.
HAMMER	It's seriously ugly.
PETAL	It's ugly like the worst of Halloween masks.
HAMMER	Nothing to say for yourself? Loser.
PETAL	And you're a dweeb!

Chewy gets angry and attempts to scare them off.

CHEWY	Leave me alone!
WISE CHORUS 4	If he gets angry and fights back,
	The bullying gets worse.
	He's sad that life is so unfair
	It feels like he's been cursed.
PETAL	No one likes you!
HAMMER	And no one wants you in their pack!

Petal and Hammer run offstage, laughing and shouting as they go. Chewy is left alone, looking dejected.

WISE CHORUS 3	Some other dogs, they run and hide
	If Chewy walks their way.
	If he sees them, they growl and shout,
	'Why don't you go away?'
PETAL *(yelling from offstage)*	Yeah, nah. No one likes you.
HAMMER *(yelling from offstage)*	Rack off, you jerk!
WISE CHORUS 4	Other dogs will pick on Chewy –
	They say his mouth is weird.
	That's not cool – it's cruel to make fun,
	Say nasty things and sneer.

| WISE CHORUS 3 | His face and body tense right up |
| | When other dogs attack. |

Chewy's body and face tense up; he looks scary.

| WISE CHORUS 4 | This threatens bullies, who are scared. |

| WISE CHORUS 1-4 | They want to pay him back. |

Chewy wanders in circles, very upset.

| CHEWY | I don't know why they're mean. |
| | I've done nothing to them … |

Wise Chorus 3 and 4 roll their eyes.

| WISE CHORUS 3 | Chewy thinks he's perfectly cool, |
| | Never making a scene. |

| WISE CHORUS 4 | But his face tells another tale – |
| | He looks cranky and mean. |

| CHEWY *(pretending)* | I don't know what to do. |
| | Anyway, I don't care … |

| WISE CHORUS 3 | Older dogs say *'Toughen up pup!'* |

| WISE CHORUS 2 | But they don't explain how. |

| WISE CHORUS 1 | They can't explain what he should do. |

| WISE CHORUS 1-4 IN UNISON | Useless advice for now! |

End of scene – music makers create sad, lonely sounds as Wise Chorus 5 and 6 enter the stage and stand in front of Wise Chorus 1-4. There is now a chorus of six students.

SCENE TWO

Tilly and Jake enter onstage. Tilly carries the leads and Jake carries dog-poop bags.

TILLY　　　　　　　　Mimi? Chewy? Time for school!

Tilly hands Jake a lead.

CHEWY　　　　　　　Oh, far out. Not again. Noooo, I wanna stay home. I've got a stomach ache.

Chewy sneaks offstage.
Mimi enters wearing a different and very sparkly collar.
Mimi rushes up to Jake, who pats her vigorously while she speaks.
Jake puts the lead on Mimi.

JAKE　　　　　　　　Good dog. Wanna go to school and have some fun?

MIMI　　　　　　　　Sure do. Can't wait to show off my new collar. *Ooh la la!* I look divine – even if I say so myself.

(with a French accent)　We French are so stylish.

TILLY　　　　　　　　Where's Chewy? Chewy?!

MIMI *(rolling her eyes)*　Do we have to wait for him?

Chewy slinks onstage.

CHEWY	Not going.
MIMI	Oh come on. I'm not being late because of you, ya dickhead.
TILLY	Mimi, that's enough with the language.
MIMI	I can't help it. It's the French in me.
TILLY	Chewy, get it together. Going to school is not negotiable. Anyway, if anyone gives you a hard time, just ignore them. Pretend it's not happening.
CHEWY	Yeah, right. Just ignore it.
JAKE	No way. I reckon he should fight back. You show them who's boss, Chewy.
CHEWY *(to himself)*	Ignore? Fight back? You two are doing my head in. And you're supposed to be the ones in charge.
MIMI *(loud whispering)*	Hey, you didn't hear this from me but sometimes our hair-parents get it wrong. Look, you might be a dickhead but you're my dickhead *frere*, so … look, there's someone at school who may be able to help you. Mrs Shetland. She's a very cool counsellor.
CHEWY	What? I'm not talking to a sheepdog. That's for losers.
MIMI	Yeah well, if the collar fits … *(pause)*

No, sorry. I don't mean that. Just keep an
open mind.
I know heaps of breeds who've been helped
by Mrs S.
She reckons managing bullies is a life skill
we all need and should work on.

JAKE   Chewy! We're going.

Chewy slinks reluctantly up to Tilly.

TILLY   Good dog.

Tilly puts a lead on Chewy.

TILLY   Who's a good dog, then?

*Tilly and Jake walk Mimi and Chewy around the stage on leads until
they arrive at 'school.' They remove the leads.*

TILLY   Here we are. Off you go, then.

CHEWY   Don't leave me!

MIMI   Don't be silly, Chewy. They'll be back at the
end of the day.
Wait here. I'll find out if Mrs S is available.

Mimi walks offstage. Chewy picks up a stick and chews on it.

CHEWY   I feel sick. Not even this stick is helping.

He howls in despair and misery.

MIMI   Here she is.
(calling from offstage)

*Mrs Shetland (Mrs S) enters the stage, energetically looking around.
She has a positive, helpful vibe.*

MRS S   What's up? Why make these miserable
sounds?

CHEWY	You don't wanna know.
MRS S	Yes I do. Come on, pup – what's up?
CHEWY *(sighing)*	Life is hard. Other dogs are mean to me.
WISE CHORUS 5	She knows that life is a puzzle: You need to get the facts,
WISE CHORUS 6	Then think and plan what you will do Before you ever act.
MRS S	What do you do about it?
CHEWY	I don't know what to do! Mum says I should ignore it …
MRS S	Uh-huh. *(pause)* How does that work out for you?
CHEWY	I try not to let it get to me, but then it does. It's in my head … and I feel like I want to throw up. So I fail at that too. *(pause)* And Dad says I should fight back.
MRS S	And how does that go?
CHEWY	Ahh, look at me. Whaddya reckon? I'm not exactly a hair-raising hound! And anyway, there's usually more than one of them, so I'm outnumbered.
MRS S	Would you be willing to try something different?
CHEWY *(shrugging)*	Suppose so. Won't help, though.
MRS S	I need to ask you, then … When they're mean and bully you, What do those dogs want *you* to do?

CHEWY *(startled)*   Whaaat?!
(pause)
What are you going on about?!!

MRS S   Think about it. As I said, 'When other dogs bully you, how do they want you to react?'

CHEWY   I dunno. Never thought about that ...

MRS S   And what do you do?
Do you walk away? Do you do 'nothing'?
Do you get freaked out?

CHEWY   Yeah, well sometimes ...
I've done all those things, I guess.
Sometimes I'm scared. Obvs.
Other times I just get really pissed off.
Sometimes I whimper.
Sometimes I run away.

MRS S   You know what? I think you become their target when you do those things.
You give them what they want.

CHEWY   Give them what they want? Are you kidding?

MRS S   I think you're giving away your power.

Riddle me this, why do you want to make these bullies happy?

Chewy is shocked and confused.

CHEWY   I don't know why,
I feel so much shame.

Mrs S nods and sighs.

MRS S *(firmly)*	It's not about shame. Bullies smell distress. They suss out your anger and your fear. They know your stressors way too well.
CHEWY	What's a stressor?
MRS S	A 'stressor' is something that causes you to feel stressed. Anything which makes you feel tense or anxious. Or that makes you feel very sensitive. It can be a situation, a person and how they behave, or something about yourself you don't like.
CHEWY	I still don't understand. What do you mean 'they know my stressors' *way too well*?
MRS S	When you get angry or cry, you're showing the bullies how *they* feel inside. It's like they're looking in a mirror. Or watching a TikTok of everything they've ever feared …
CHEWY	That's weird. I didn't know bullies got afraid or scared …
MRS S	Of course they do. They're like the rest of us – even though they pretend to be tough.
WISE CHORUS 6	Chewy felt strange and quite surprised trashing these false beliefs. If he could take on the bullies,
WISE CHORUS 1–6 IN UNISON	What a massive relief.

End of scene – music makers make sounds reflecting Chewy's confusion.

SCENE THREE

Wise Chorus on stage to the side. Mrs S and Chewy are centre stage.

MRS S   But don't take my word for it. Let's ask someone who's had paws-on experience. I did some counselling with Diesel the Doberman last year.
Get yourself out here, Diesel!

(calls loudly)   Diesel!

CHEWY *(frightened)*   No way! A Doberman!

MRS S   Don't be like that. Diesel's a real softie once you get to know him. And he had to deal with some nasty cyber bullying from Chi Chi the Chihuahua.

Diesel strolls onto the stage wearing sunglasses.

DIESEL   You called?

MRS S   Ooh, like your sunnies.

DIESEL   Ta, Mrs S. Got them from Vinnies. Anyway, wassup?

MRS S   Chewy here is being bullied. And he gives them what they're looking for.

	He doesn't mean to, but when they pester him, he gives them just the reaction they want – by getting angry, scared or sad.
DIESEL	*Pfft.* You gotta stop doing that. You gotta learn to manage your feelings.
MRS S	Well, go on. Tell him how. He's not a mind reader.
DIESEL	It boils down to getting in touch with your inner mammal. You need to be able to identify your feelings. That might sound hard, but there are only four main feelings – glad, sad, mad and bad.
MRS S	Which is why they're used so much as emojis ...
DIESEL	Once you know *what* you're feeling, you can stop being so frightened of those big emotions and learn to manage them. Then you can start to change your reactions.
MRS S	Great advice, Diesel. And how do you suggest Chewy changes his reactions?
DIESEL	Hmmm. I always look my fellow dogs in the eye.

Removes his sunglasses.

DIESEL *(continued)*	Take these off first, of course.
MRS S	Though there are some dogs who avoid eye contact as a matter of courtesy. It's the culture of their breed.

DIESEL	Too true, Mrs S. And if that's the case, well, I respect that. What I'm saying here is: I like to take my time and not rush in. I check those doggies out. I make sure they're kind and friendly, and I avoid the nasty ones.
MRS S	Spot on, Diesel.
CHEWY *(unconvinced)*	Yeah, okay.
DIESEL	As I said, I watch each dog closely. Are they friendly to everyone? If so, that's cool. But if they're nice to most but mean to some, I steer clear of them. Be discerning, my friend. *Discerning.*
CHEWY *(confused)*	*Diss* what?
DIESEL	Dis-cern-ing.
MRS S	It means to use good judgment. Use your common sense to work out who's worth being your friend.
DIESEL	Exactly. Some animals are friendly one day, mean the next. Stay away from those who keep changing their mind. Stick to those who are reliable. And kind. Like me.
CHEWY	Gotcha. I think …

Chewy slouches, still somewhat dejected.
Mellow the Retriever bounces onstage.

DIESEL	Hey here's Mellow. Let's find out what they think. Whaddya reckon, Mellow?

	How do you manage your fears if someone's hassling you?
MELLOW	My approach is physical. When I stand up straight, I breathe more deeply. It makes me feel confident and I find I speak more clearly. That works for me.
DIESEL	Yeaaaah. I like that. Using your body to help your brain.
MELLOW	You need to look cool and calm. Don't jiggle about. I don't mean to stereotype, but your average terrier finds this very difficult to follow. But as a retriever, I'm even-tempered and I know how to hide what I feel inside if I need to. That way, I don't give bullies the satisfaction of seeing how I really feel.
MRS S	Exactly. Aim to keep a neutral face. Don't show them that you're upset.
MELLOW *(to Chewy)*	I mean this in the kindest way, but you should stop slouching. You're giving off baaad vibes.

Chewy stands up straighter.

CHEWY	But what if I get attacked? You know, physically?
DIESEL	Don't put up with that. Report it.
CHEWY	Then they'll say I'm a dobber. And threaten to bash me when no-one's around.

DIESEL	It's a no-brainer. You have to report physical bullying. Don't try to fight back.
CHEWY	But my hair-Dad reckons I should stand up for myself and fight back!
MELLOW	Nah, that's seriously old school. No disrespect to your hair-Dad – I'm sure he's really nice and everything – but that advice is outdated. There are smarter ways. Using your mind, not your paws.
DIESEL	Spot on, Mellow. You can't change anyone else. Only yourself. And your attitude.
CHEWY	But what if someone says, 'You don't belong'? What if there's a group and no one wants to include me?
DIESEL	Forget them! Who wants to be part of a group that's so mean. Find dogs who ask, 'You want to join in?' *(pause)* Look, Chewy, I do appreciate it's not always as simple as that. Sometimes dogs bully without meaning to and sometimes other dogs go along with the bullying because it's easier not to rock the kennel. Doesn't mean they agree with it.
CHEWY	And what if someone abuses me on my socials?
DIESEL	Block them! Literally! A social 'friend' who abuses you online is not a real friend.

WISE CHORUS 5   Chewy listened and he absorbed
The ideas offered up.
He still felt pretty freaked out though
A frightened, wary pup.

WISE CHORUS 6   But he agreed to try new ways
And test them for himself.
He told himself: *don't worry mate.*

WISE CHORUS 1 – 6   *Dump those fears on the shelf!*
IN UNISON

End of scene – music makers create loud, upbeat, positive sounds.

SCENE FOUR

Wise Chorus onstage to the side.

Mimi and Chewy are hanging out onstage when Petal and Hammer trot in.

Mrs S is watching from the sidelines in view of the audience.

CHEWY   You're kidding me. Just my luck.

HAMMER *(friendly)*   Hey, Mimi ... Love your outfit. Wanna play?

MIMI *(confidently)*   Nah, I'm busy. Got ball-catching practice.

Mimi exits the stage.
Sunny and Mango bounce onstage and sniff with friendliness at the other dogs.

SUNNY   Gidday everyone! Isn't it a beautiful day?

HAMMER   Sure is, Sunny.
                                   (pauses for effect)
                                   Get it? I made a joke. I said, 'Sure is, Sunny.'
                                   And it's a sunny day.
                                   And I was talking to you, Sunny.

MANGO *(kindly)*   Not one of your best, Hammer.

PETAL *(disdainfully)*   Pathetic. As bad as my hair-Dad's jokes.

HAMMER   Yeah?

Hammer barks at Petal. They have a friendly fight, barking and roughhousing together.
Sunny and Mango move out of the way to the other side of the stage.
Hammer and Petal stop their play fight, panting with the exertion.

PETAL	Jeez, that was fun. What's next?

Hammer notices Chewy.

HAMMER *(menacingly)*	Well helloooo, Chewy. Seems you're on your lonesome today. That's okay. We'll play with you. Won't we, Petal?

PETAL *(scarily)*	Yeah, we'd love to play.

Hammer and Petal circle Chewy. Chewy slouches. He's intimidated.

PETAL *(pretending to* *be interested)*	Did you know I'm a fourth-generation pit-bull terrier? Tell me Chewy, what breed are you again?

CHEWY	I'm not sure. I was a rescue.

HAMMER	But what do your breeding papers say? My father was Best in Show last year at the Easter Fair. My papers trace my Rottweiler ancestors back 30 years.

CHEWY	I don't have papers.

PETAL	You must have come from somewhere.

CHEWY	I came from my mother.

Hammer and Petal laugh.

PETAL	Hilarious. He came from his mother! Basic!! But what's your pedigree, you nutjob?

Chewy shrugs.

PETAL *(continued)*	And what exactly is wrong with your teeth?
CHEWY	I was born like this.
HAMMER	They're the most disgusting teeth I've ever seen. You're an embarrassment to the entire dog race. Did your mouth get switched at birth? With a scarecrow!
PETAL	No – with a witch!

Hammer and Petal laugh again. They find themselves very amusing.

CHEWY	Don't be mean. I can't help it.
HAMMER *(mimicking)*	Don't be mean.
CHEWY *(upset)*	It's not my fault.
PETAL	Oooh. You really got me, Chewy.
HAMMER	You're not only ugly, you're stupid too.
CHEWY	Don't call me stupid! Just cause I'm a rescue doesn't mean ... *(his lip starts to quiver)*
PETAL	Oh look he's gonna start whimpering ... what a cry-puppy.
CHEWY *(suddenly angry)*	Get lost! All of you. Get lost!

Chewy barks and howls furiously.

HAMMER *(mocking)*	Jeez, you're really scaring me, Chewy.
PETAL	This is boring. You can stop already. We're out of here.

Hammer and Petal leave the stage.
Chewy continues to bark furiously – this time at Sunny and Mango.

CHEWY　　　　　　　Both of you too! Go away!

Sunny and Mango are confused and frightened. They rush away in fear.
Chewy's barking reduces, his anger dissipates and he looks miserable.

MRS S *(kindly)*　　　You okay?

CHEWY *(cranky)*　　　Obviously not.

Chewy takes a deep breath.

CHEWY　　　　　　　Sorry, Mrs S. I didn't mean to be rude.
　　　　　　　　　　　I know you're trying to help. But I messed
　　　　　　　　　　　up. Again. And now no-one's gonna be
　　　　　　　　　　　my friend.

MRS S　　　　　　　*I'm* in your corner Chewy. And yes, you
　　　　　　　　　　　did mess up.
　　　　　　　　　　　BUT … on the other hand, you tried.
　　　　　　　　　　　You should pat yourself on the back for that.

Chewy pats himself on the back.

CHEWY *(sarcastically)* Good dog, Chewy.

MRS S　　　　　　　Come on. I mean it.
　　　　　　　　　　　It's never easy when you're learning new
　　　　　　　　　　　skills, new ways of reacting. It takes time.
　　　　　　　　　　　And practice.
　　　　　　　　　　　One thing I know for sure is that you're not
　　　　　　　　　　　helping yourself by being a bully to yourself.
　　　　　　　　　　　We need to work on building your
　　　　　　　　　　　confidence … and that means in here.
　　　　　　　　　　　(taps her head)

Mrs S puts her arm around Chewy and leads him offstage.

WISE CHORUS 1	Some dogs believe their breed is best – Tease all those not the same.
WISE CHORUS 2	They say that they're just joking you, But that's a nasty game.
WISE CHORUS 3	Other dogs say it's in good fun, They're just messing about,
WISE CHORUS 4	But watch how they treat each other: That shows you without doubt.
WISE CHORUS 5	Some bullies attack in a group – Don't face them on your own.
WISE CHORUS 6	Reach out to get support and help: You shouldn't be alone.

End of scene – music makers create positive sounds.

SCENE FIVE

Wise Chorus onstage to the side.

Ziggy the greyhound enters doing a zoomie around the stage.

Mrs S follows with Chewy.

MRS S   Hey, there's Ziggy. I bet she can help.
                      She had a tough time before she was
                      rescued and yet she's made friends
                      with *everyone*.
                      Ziggy! This is Chewy.

Chewy and Ziggy circle and sniff each other in a friendly way.

MRS S *(to Ziggy)*   He gets teased a lot and it's really getting
                      him down.

ZIGGY   Sorry to hear that.

MRS S   Got any suggestions?

ZIGGY   Back when I was racing, it could get really
                      competitive.
                      Some of the other hounds tried mental
                      tactics to unnerve me before a race.
                      You know, like, try to get inside my head
                      and put me off.
                      Intense stuff.

MRS S	And what did you do about it?
ZIGGY	I found the best way was to use simple comebacks. You know the kind of thing – retorts. Retorts to block them. So, if they said something nasty to me, I'd politely reply with 'And?' and not show them it was getting to me.
MRS S	Yes, that's important – keeping a neutral face and not looking upset. Don't give away your power.
ZIGGY	Exactly. Other times, if they insulted me, I'd agree with them! I'd say, 'Thanks' or 'Nobody's perfect.' And that would give them such a surprise, it put *them* off balance.
CHEWY *(sceptical)*	Does that really work?
ZIGGY	In my experience it does. Bullies don't know what to say or do when you take away their power. For example; if one of them told me I wasn't fast enough and was never going to win a race, then I'd say, 'You're right. But I'm getting a lot better. And practising every day.' That usually shut them up. Actually, they often got embarrassed and treated me with more respect after that.
MRS S	Let's practise some retorts!
CHEWY	No way ... I can never think of anything clever to say.

MRS S	You don't have to be clever. And you don't have to think of something in the heat of the moment. You need to practise, that's all. But tell you what – to get you started, we'll show you how. We'll do a role play. I'll pretend to be a bully, and Ziggy, you can give Chewy some good retorts. Ready, Zig?

Ziggy nods.

MRS S *(continued)*	Here we go. Hey Ziggy, you're offending my eyes. You fat slob!
ZIGGY *(surprised)*	Seriously, Mrs S. Me? Fat? I've got the metabolism of a greyhound. I'm built like a whippet!
MRS S	It's a *role play*, Ziggy. Just pretend. Get with the program.

Chewy watches on with interest.

ZIGGY	Gotcha. Hypothetical role-play. Hit me again.
MRS S	Hey Ziggy, I said you're fat!
ZIGGY	No, I'm not. I'm *ginormous*!
MRS S	Well done. Great comeback. Let's try another one. How about, 'You're an idiot!'
ZIGGY	Nah, not today. Yesterday I was an idiot. Today I'm just stupid.

MRS S	So you admit you're ginormous and stupid. Well guess what? You're ugly too.
ZIGGY *(shrugging)*	Yeah? And I'm good at sleeping. I'm not called a couch potato for nothing.
MRS S	See what he's doing, Chewy? Let's try a harder one …
	Yuck, keep away from me – you're gay!
ZIGGY	So what? It's not catching. And I like liver treats. Get over it.
MRS S	Well, your fur's too dark!
ZIGGY	I might look different to you, but beneath my fur we're exactly the same. And my farts are just like yours.
CHEWY *(with admiration)*	That's dank, Zig!
ZIGGY	No more than you can be!

Ziggy runs offstage and calls back loudly.

You just need to *practise!!*

Chewy and Mrs S follow him offstage.

WISE CHORUS 6	So, practise retorts to block them:
WISE CHORUS 5	'And?' 'Thanks.' 'No-one's perfect.' Practise, practise, practise, practise
WISE CHORUS 5 & 6	Until you can't forget!

Wise Chorus 5 and 6 high-five each other.

WISE CHORUS 4	Learn some good replies and comebacks Try them out day by day

WISE CHORUS 3	Or practise using a smart phone, Then they're easy to say.
WISE CHORUS 2	Remember this rule of friendship: Kids like those they respect.
WISE CHORUS 1	When you help to block a bully You help all kids connect.
WISE CHORUS 5	But if they're still mean or nasty,
WISE CHORUS 2	Freeze up your face like ice.
WISE CHORUS 4	Don't look at them or say a word,
WISE CHORUS 1-6 *in unison*	Avoid them like they're lice!
WISE CHORUS 6	Sometimes they don't appreciate
WISE CHORUS 1	Bullying causes pain.
WISE CHORUS 3	And, if it goes on for too long
WISE CHORUS 1-6 **IN UNISON**	Will really harm your brain!

End of scene – music makers make discordant sounds.

SCENE SIX

Wise Chorus onstage to the side.

Mrs S and Chewy walk onstage, talking as they enter and arrive centre front.

Chewy carries a phone in his pocket.

MRS S   It's your turn now, Chewy.
Ziggy's given you some ideas, but you must practise. And not just in your head.
Say them out loud.
In front of a mirror.
Or, if you can, record them on a device and play them back so you can see what works and what needs improving.
Get out your phone.

Chewy takes out his phone.

CHEWY   Ah, okay. But this feels weird.

Chewy starts recording himself self-consciously, jiggling around.

CHEWY *(continued)*   'Nobody's perfect but getting there is my next project.'

MRS S   And remember your body language. Stand up straight. Don't jiggle or wiggle.

Chewy straightens up, stops jiggling. He stands with straight shoulders practising his neutral face in the phone screen. Mrs S watches on.

MRS S *(continued)* I've got another tip for you. Ever heard of a square smile?

CHEWY Can't say I have.

MRS S You'll find it very useful to block connections, especially those from a bully. Put on a fake smile by stretching your lips into a square. And show your teeth – both top and bottom rows.

Mrs S demonstrates. Chewy copies her.

CHEWY There's so much to remember!

MRS S You're doing a great job. And don't let your eyes smile. Keep them blank and cold as ice. You can flash this square grin whenever you feel the need to keep someone at paw's length.

Chewy practices his square smile on the phone.
Mimi slinks onstage into Chewy's view. She's obviously upset.

CHEWY Mimi, what's wrong? Are you sick?

MIMI No, I'm fine.

CHEWY You really don't seem fine, Mimi.
Everything I see is telling me you're upset.
Your tail's between your legs and your ears are flat.
Your body is showing me you're sad.
What's happened?

MIMI	Oh Chewy, you're right. I'm trapped in a living nightmare! Chi Chi is spreading lies about me online. She's posted that I've got fleas and now everyone is making fun of me!
CHEWY	I thought you two were besties ...
MIMI	We were. But she's become so up herself since she got selected for the Gifted and Talented Agility program. She's a skanky bitch and I told her so!
CHEWY	'kay. And how'd that work out for you?
MIMI	She said I was just jealous. *Moi!* Jealous? As if! And then she posted I was a sore loser.
CHEWY	I'm not surprised. You gave her what she wanted. Believe me, I know exactly how awful it feels to give away your power. But first things first. *(pause)* Is it true? Do you have fleas?
MIMI	Of course not! *(scratches)* Maybe just one or two. Our hair-parents were a few days late with my flea powder.
CHEWY	One or two fleas is nothing to be ashamed of.
MIMI	Maybe for you! But for *moi* ... it's a catastrophe! It's the French in me. We have such high grooming standards.

CHEWY	Mimi, take a chill pill. I'm gonna make a suggestion. Mellow taught me some skills he says are a no-brainer.
MIMI	Perfect for you then!
CHEWY	Funny. Do you want my help or not?
MIMI	Suppose it wouldn't kill me to listen.
CHEWY	Right. Next time Chi Chi says awful things about you, instead of calling her something rude, how about you try saying something like 'Thanks for letting me know' using a neutral voice of course. And give her a square smile. In fact, make all your face neutral – unreadable – so you don't show her how you're feeling inside.

Chewy demonstrates the square smile and neutral face.

MIMI	What? How do you ... Okay then ...
CHEWY	I promise it works. And if Chi Chi continues, then block her. Literally. Who needs a friend like that! You've got lots of IRL friends and you're worth a hundred Chi Chi's to me.
MIMI	Awww, thanks Chewy. That's so sweet. I do feel a little bit better. Though I'm kinda surprised a rescue like you knows all this clever *merde*.

She walks offstage much happier.

CHEWY	Thanks. *(pause)* I think.

MRS S   Nice one, Chewy. You're getting the hang
                                  of this.

Sniffs loudly.

MRS S *(continued)*   Did you fart?

Comrade the Labrador wanders on.

COMRADE   Did someone mention farting? I'm the boss
                                  of farting.

MRS S   You're telling me. Thank goodness there's a
                                  breeze.

COMRADE *(pleased)*   I know. I'm legendary.

MRS S   From what I've seen, you're also a legend at
                                  making friends.

Chewy's attention wanders. He pulls out his phone and scrolls.

COMRADE   I find that most dogs are nice to me because
                                  I smile and wag my tail. They know they'll
                                  have fun with me. We labradors are famous
                                  for our friendly natures.

MRS S   Chewy, listen up! Get off that device!!
                                  Comrade's giving you her insights here;
                                  don't be so rude.

Chewy keeps scrolling.

COMRADE   And I always ask the best questions.
                                  I'm proud of my farts but I'm even prouder
                                  of my ability to help those who feel left out.

MRS S   Really, Chewy? I'm only going to say it once
                                  more. Get off that screen!!

Chewy stops scrolling and focuses on Mrs S.

	There's no reason you can't be like Comrade. Actually, we should all try to be like Comrade. She's the GOAT of making friends.
WISE CHORUS 4	She's the G-O-A-T for sure And you can be like her If you follow the tips offered Regardless of your fur.
WISE CHORUS 2	A friendly greeting cannot fail: You simply say hello Then smile and look them in the eye. Let your friendliness show.
WISE CHORUS 6	Show your interest in one and all Listen with a 'noddie'.

Wise Chorus all nod to demonstrate

WISE CHORUS 6	Make sure you're not distracted, though, In your mind or body.
WISE CHORUS 3	Give them your complete attention, Don't get stuck on your phone. Be fully present for your friends, So no-one feels alone.
WISE CHORUS 5	Have questions ready you can ask, That work for everyone. Ask about their favourite hobbies, Like friends, sports, apps and fun.
WISE CHORUS 1	Chewy absorbed all the advice His new friends offered up. He practised these smart skills at length – His confidence went up!

End of scene – music makers create confident sounds!

SCENE SEVEN

Wise Chorus are on stage to the side.

Mrs S and Chewy are downstage in the middle.

MRS S Chewy, now you've mastered retorts and the square smile, it's time for the next step.

CHEWY Whaaat, there's more?

MRS S There is. But first, let's recap.

CHEWY This feels just like school.

MRS S Maybe so, but it might be the most important thing you learn all year.
So, suck it up, pup, and listen.
Science has proven that bullying changes your brain.
Damages it.
That's why I'm harping on about managing bullies – because it's an important life skill. This might surprise you, but it can happen at any time of your life. And when it does, it's simply not possible to ignore – you'd be inhuman if you weren't affected by it.

CHEWY *(sarcastically)* But we're dogs, not humans.

MRS S It's a figure of speech, Chewy.
And you know exactly what I mean.
Which is why you have to learn not to show fear or worry or anger.
Use retorts to show it's not getting to you.
Then the next step is to reprogram yourself.
Change your attitude and become a better communicator.
Those things will help you navigate *everything* in life *and* attract friends.
Remember, you cannot change other dogs.
You can only change yourself: your own response and your own attitude.
But take heart. There is great power in that.

Petal and Hammer come belting onto the stage. Chewy looks frightened but then straightens his shoulders.

MRS S That's it, pup. You can handle this.
Remember to breathe deeply!

Mrs S moves upstage.

PETAL Ah, if it isn't our little friend Chewy with the effed-up teeth …

HAMMER How's it going today, Chewy?
You do know that your shit-ugly mouth is still the prettiest part of you, don't ya?

Chewy takes a deep breath, stands up straight and looks confident.

CHEWY Tell me something I don't know.
But actually, I think my paws are the worst part of me.
My teeth may be rotten but my paws are putrid.

HAMMER	Say what?
CHEWY	You heard me.

Chewy gives a square, neutral smile and stands tall without jiggling or moving around.

PETAL	So you're agreeing you're ugly?
CHEWY	Oh yes, I completely agree. I'm beyond ugly. I am without doubt the ugliest dog in the park. So what? And now I need to fart.

Petal and Hammer are dumbstruck.

PETAL	I'm not hanging with this gross critter. Coming, Hammer?
HAMMER	In a mo. I'll catch up with you.

Petal leaves, somewhat confused about this turn of events.

CHEWY	Can I help you with anything, Hammer?
HAMMER	No ... well, yes. I'm sorry about that ugly mouth shit, I got carried away. Do you wanna hang out? *(pause)* We could play 'sniff my gastric output'.
CHEWY	You mean 'sniff my poo'?
HAMMER	Yeah. But I'm tryna be respectful.
CHEWY	I'm free at lunchtime tomorrow if you wanna sniff my gastric output then.
HAMMER	Okay. See you tomorrow!

Hammer runs offstage. Chewy gives a quiet smile of satisfaction.

WISE CHORUS 1   Chewy could tell that it had worked –
The tactics he had used.
The bullies were dumbstruck, you see:
He made them feel confused.

WISE CHORUS 2   He didn't react to their words,
Which gave them quite a shock.
He felt strong, and in charge again
Using the bully block.

WISE CHORUS 3   These days he plays with lots of friends
He's kind yet assertive.
He's friendly but no pushover
He's Mr Positive!

WISE CHORUS 4   He still does make mistakes at times
But says 'No need for fits'.
He uses self-talk to calm down
'What can I learn from this?'

WISE CHORUS 5   So if you ever get bullied
Now or when you're older,
Remember Chewy and his friends
You too can be bolder.

WISE CHORUS 6   Regard this as a game to play,
Don't make bullies happy.
Don't show them that they bother you,
Don't be scared or snappy.

WISE CHORUS 1   Instead, look them straight in the eye
And put on a blank face.

WISE CHORUS 2   Or if you'd rather block them out,
Stare blankly into space.

WISE CHORUS 3   If they are being mean to you,
Just say 'And?' 'What?' or 'Thanks!'

WISE CHORUS 4	Use a neutral comeback like that Or have fun with word pranks.
WISE CHORUS 5	Remember, everybody likes A friendly, caring face.
WISE CHORUS 6	If you wear one, you might well find Connections taking place.

Tilly and Jake walk onstage during the last verse and go up to Chewy, patting him affectionately.

WISE CHORUS 1 & 2	You don't need to suffer alone,
WISE CHORUS 3 & 4	Find friendly dogs out there.
WISE CHORUS 5 & 6	Do some noddies, and add a smile,
ALL WISE CHORUS	Your social life will flare!
TILLY	Did you notice Chewy playing with Hammer today? I never thought I'd see that. Chewy, you did great in the park today. We're so proud of you.
JAKE	Yes, we are. Ooh, we are. Good dog, good dog. Who's a good dog, then?
CHEWY *(mimicking)*	'Good dog, good dog.'

Chewy gives the audience a huge smile and a victory salute.

| CHEWY *(continued)* | It's time to call me *great* dog! |

The music makers erupt into loud, joyful celebratory sounds!

THE END

THE BULLY BLOCKER RESOURCES

SCENE ONE

Cast

- Chewy
- Mimi
- Tilly
- Jake
- Sunny
- Mango
- Petal
- Hammer
- Wise Chorus 1–4
- Music makers

Props

- Collars × 6
- Leads × 2
- Dog bowls × 2
- Kibble
- Hairbrush

Precis

We meet the main characters, Chewy and Mimi, and their hair-parents – Tilly and Jake.

Mimi is a purebred French poodle and a supremely confident character.

Chewy is an adopted dog of indeterminate, mixed breed. He is sweet and kind in nature but exceptionally shy and socially fearful.

Chewy struggles to join in socially and behaves inappropriately in what should be friendly, uncomplicated interactions.

Petal and Hammer delight in ridiculing Chewy's mouth and he reacts with anger and fear.

The Wise Chorus explain the many ways Chewy gets bullied and how his body and mind react.

Concept: What is bullying?

Bullying is an abuse of power. It is not 'just jokes' or 'just teasing', though bullies will often defend themselves or try to deflect that that's all it is. Regardless of intent, bullying is distressing and harmful.

It involves hurtful physical, psychological, social and virtual behaviours. It is most commonly experienced from ages 8 to 16 at school but also happens in sport, the community, during tertiary education and in the workplace.

Kids can be bullied by peers, younger or older students.

It varies from subtle to forceful behaviours, from teasing to physical abuse, from 'just having fun' to criminal behaviours.

It can occur once, occasionally or constantly.

It can be one-on-one or be perpetrated by a mob – where a group targets an individual. The mob often has a leader or small group who control the situation.

Whatever form it takes and however often it happens, the outcome is the same. It is hugely damaging. Someone gets hurt and can quickly lose belief in themselves as a worthy, valued member of society.

We are social beings and need to belong to a group, tribe or family to survive. When that inclusion is threatened through bullying, the individual is profoundly harmed and the group is weaker for it.

🗨 Discussion prompts

What is bullying?

Is bullying different from teasing, ribbing, jokes?

How? Why?

When does 'joking' turn into bullying?

Is bullying something that happens only at school?

If not, where else does bullying happen?

Are you surprised to learn that adults can be bullied?

Concept: Types of bullying

There are five main types of bullying and all are harmful.

1. Verbal

Teasing is the most toxic, harmful type of bullying. Mean words stick in the target's brain and are ruminated on – over and over. This can scar the target's brain forever. Most common forms of teasing are about

- Appearance
- Intelligence
- Gender
- Social approval

The tease hurts because of the bully's mean manner, tone, facial expressions, repetition and what the tease means to the target and their peers.

But – it's all about social context.

For example, in one school wearing braces may be seen as ugly ('metal mouth, brace face, train tracks') but in another school wearing braces may be a status symbol.

Note that the effect of this type of bullying is usually very different to that of teasing by siblings or close family members. A child may laugh or not take it that personally if their brother, sister or cousin calls them an idiot. There is often banter in families that does not have the same impact as school bullying. If a peer says the same thing ('You're an idiot', 'You're pathetic'), the bullied child may feel attacked on a deep level.

2. Exclusion

When the bully manipulates the group to isolate the target.

It can be direct ('You can't sit with us', 'This seat is reserved for cool people only') – to indirect, using subtle, non-verbal body language (turning their backs on the target, placing bags on a seat to stop the target using it).

The goal of exclusion is to create a group identity which becomes a powerful control mechanism. Each group member knows that if they support the target, they'll be next to be evicted. So even a target's friends may not have the fortitude to stand up to the bully.

When a bully is devious and has a well-developed bullying skill set, the teacher's presence is irrelevant. A bully's raised eyebrow or silent gesture behind the teacher's back may be enough to frighten the target. Because, as teachers, you are not blessed with the superpower of being omnipotent, you may miss this indirect aggression.

3. Physical

Involves attacking someone less powerful. It can be directly aggressive, such as hitting, kicking or spitting, or indirect such as by gesture, suggestions, stalking, damaging or hiding property. It can include grabbing the target by their clothing and ripping it. Or provoking a fight in which the target is defenceless.

4. Harassment and discrimination

Involves repeated, annoying questions, statements or attacks about the target's:

- Gender
- Sexuality
- Race
- Religion
- Nationality
- Etc.

The aim is to exclude the target for being different.

5. Cyberbullying

'... occurs when a person is repeatedly mean, nasty, horrible, harassing and/or threatening to another person using any internet site, game application, or platform and/or via mobile phone.' (Susan McLean, cyber safety expert, 2023)

💬 Discussion prompts

What are the main types of bullying?

Which type of bullying is worse? Or are they all as bad as each other?

Why?

In the first scene we see Chewy being teased by the other dogs.

Why is Chewy bullied?

How do you think Chewy feels about being bullied?

What internal reactions does it foster in him?

Which of the following do you think Chewy feels?

- Embarrassment
- Shame
- Like a failure
- Humiliation
- Self-critical
- Low confidence
- Abnormal
- Angry
- Confused
- Blames himself

Sunny and Mango are friendly dogs, yet Chewy still won't trust them or play with them.

Why do you think that happens?

Why has Chewy become distrustful of everyone?

In Scene One Mimi teases her brother Chewy a number of times – yet she quickly supported him when he needed it. Is teasing within a family (including banter and inside-jokes) different from bullying?

When does family banter or teasing become bullying?

Activity: Where does it fit?

Write up two headings – 'Bullying Behaviour' and 'Harmless Behaviour'

Photocopy the list of behaviours below, cut into individual sections and place in a container.

Each student picks an example and reads it out aloud to the class.

They nominate which heading they think the behaviour sits under and explain their reasoning.

The rest of the class decides whether or not they agree with the classification and adds any different perspectives or interpretations.

The activity will highlight that some behaviours are obviously bullying.

Other behaviours will depend on the context.

List of behaviour examples

Note – some examples may need to be edited out as they may not be age appropriate for your class. Add some examples of your own which are relevant to your class situation.

1. Hitting a class member with a ruler
2. Commenting on someone's Instagram that their post is suss
3. Saying to another student, 'You can't sit here. Only cool people are allowed to sit here.'
4. Giving the middle finger to someone

5. Grabbing your crutch and thrusting your pelvis at someone

6. Pulling someone's hair

7. Saying to another student, 'Jeez you're lucky, your mum is so hot.'

8. Flicking your towel at someone when you're in the sports change room

9. Saying to another student 'You run like a girl ...'

10. Pushing in ahead of someone in the canteen queue

11. Saying to another student 'F*ck off, you stink.'

12. Tagging a fellow student on your Intsa and posting 'Check out this guy. World's biggest dickhead.'

13. Deliberately running into someone in the corridor and then saying 'Sorry' in an exaggerated, sarcastic way

14. Posting a photograph of someone without their permission

15. Saying to an Indigenous Australian student, 'Hey monkey, where's your banana?'

16. Saying to a group of students about another student, 'He wants to be my boyfriend, but he's got no chance.'

17. Saying to someone in your friendship group, 'Don't get so upset, I was just kidding about your nose hijacking your face.'

18. Saying to someone outside your friendship group, 'Don't get so upset, I was just kidding about your nose hijacking your face.'

19. Grabbing another student's bag and throwing it across the playground

20. Saying to a student, 'Go back to where you came from.'

21. Posting a photograph of a classmate which shows part of their body naked

22. Saying to a classmate, 'You're so nice to everyone it makes me want to puke.'

23. Saying to another student, 'You're awesome.'

24. Saying to a classmate, 'How do you even say your name? It's so weird, so long and so many vowels. Your parents are obviously not real Aussies.'

25. Saying to another student, 'What kind of a name is Mohammed anyway? My Dad says your family are terrorists.'

26. Saying to a classmate during Phys Ed, 'You might be the GOAT at maths but when I see you try to shoot a hoop ... epic fail.'

27. Saying to a classmate, 'I bet you don't need sunscreen. Not with skin that colour.'

28. Saying to a younger student, 'Give me your lunch money or you know what will happen ...'

29. Stealing a cap from another student's bag

30. Saying to a classmate, 'Give me the answers to the maths homework. Now, or I'll have to tell everyone you wet the bed.'

31. Deliberately tearing another student's uniform

Concept: Who gets bullied?

Absolutely, without exception, anyone can. This is not meant to frighten anyone. It's meant to highlight that there is no shame in being a target because it can happen to anyone. This is clear from the following two examples.

Example 1 – Catherine, the Princess of Wales, was bullied in Year 7.

Kate Middleton, as she was known then, briefly went to a prestigious girls' school where she was targeted over her appearance and reputation 'as quite a soft and nice person'. After she was bullied, it affected her so badly she changed schools.

Her experience was so traumatic that when she married Prince William, they asked their guests that in lieu of gifts, they donate money to charities – including one that helps people who are bullied.

Example 2 – Michael Phelps, the now retired American swimmer is the most successful and most decorated Olympian of all time. He holds

28 medals and the all-time records for Olympic Gold medals. And he was bullied when he was younger.

He shared his experience in a documentary called *Angst* where he revealed he was bullied because of his long limbs and big ears. This made him very depressed and lead to severe anxiety.

💬 Discussion prompts

Were you surprised to learn about the experiences of seemingly confident and high-achieving adults like Princess Catherine and Michel Phelps?

How does learning about their experiences make you feel?

Michael Phelps was bullied because of his noticeably long limbs. Yet that same body feature helped him become an Olympic champion. What do you make of that observation?

Activity: Research a celebrity!

In small groups, research a famous person or celebrity who has talked about being bullied. Research the type of bullying they experienced and how it affected them.

Report your findings back to the class as if you are delivering a short news item on the evening news.

Suggestions of people to research:

Dylan Alcott	Justin Beiber	Tiger Woods
Taylor Swift	Chris Rock	Justin Timberlake
Eva Mendes	Kate Winslett	Lorde
Lady Gaga	Latrell Mitchell	Adam Goodes
Drake	Priyanka Chopra	Christian Bale
Jackie Chan	Ed Sheeran	Robert Pattinson
Tom Cruise	Rhianna	Melissa Wu

Concept: Where does bullying occur?

In a nutshell, everywhere.

Anywhere in the world and in any type of school: poor, wealthy, private, state, co-ed, single sex, small, large, religious, non-sectarian, conservative, traditional, progressive, day, boarding, city, country, preschool, primary school, high school, technical, tertiary.

And it occurs wherever students congregate in groups – in class, on the playground, at the canteen, in toilets, at lockers, in change rooms, on the sports field, in isolated corridors, on school camp, walking to and from school, on public transport, at out of hours school care programs, at local shopping centres and online.

Bullying escalates in stressful cultures where everyone competes to succeed or where a higher status predominates.

🗨 Discussion prompts

We see Chewy being bullied at home by visiting dogs, Petal and Hammer.

His hair-parents are not there when it happens.

Do you think that parents/adults always know when bullying happens?

Why or why not?

Imagine you've been bullied at school (or perhaps you don't have to imagine because it's happened to you).

How comfortable do you feel talking to your parents about the experience? Why or why not?

How comfortable do you feel talking to your teacher about the experience? Why or why not?

What needs to change to help you feel comfortable reporting or discussing bullying with an adult you trust?

Concept: The roles in the bullying game

There are three roles when the bully game is played:

1. Bully – the person who does the bullying
2. Target – the victim of the bullying behaviour
3. Bystanders – those who witness the bullying

Bullies

We have discussed in earlier exercises the broad range of behaviour that bullying can entail. The key point to remember is that all types of bullying are harmful.

Targets

If targeted people betray their true feelings – fear, distress, anger – they make themselves more of a target. Even if kids claim they did nothing, their anxiety is reflected in their voice, body language, and words. They freeze, turn away or look upset, scared or angry. This feeds the bully's power.

Their reactions show the bully that their bullying has worked and has paid off – the game (aka cycle) continues.

Bystanders

There are three possible reactions by bystanders. They may:

1. Stay silent
2. Participate
3. Stand up to and challenge the bully about their behaviour (when a bystander challenges a bully they become an upstander)

🗨 Discussion prompts

When Chewy is teased by Petal and Hammer, his face and body tense up and he looks scary and intimidating.

The Wise Chorus comments on this saying:

Chewy thinks he's perfectly cool,

Never making a scene
But his face tells another tale –
He looks cranky and mean.

What story does Chewy's face tell the other dogs?

How do you think the friendly dogs Sunny and Mango feel about Chewy's reactions?

What reactions does he give which encourage Petal and Hammer to keep targeting him?

Do you personally know of others whose lives were affected by bullying at school?

How did it affect them?

Activity: Self-reflection

Reflect on the questions in Worksheet A and write your answers.

Self-reflection

Answer the following questions. There are no right or wrong responses. Your answers are private and for self-reflection.

1. What types of bullying have you witnessed recently?

_____

_____

_____

2. Did you join in?

_____

_____

3. How did you react to watching someone else be bullied? Did you do anything about it?

_____

_____

4. Have you been bullied lately? If so, how did you react to being bullied?

_____

_____

_____

5. Do you bully any of your fellow students/friends? If so, why do you think that is?

_____

_____

SCENE TWO

Cast

- Chewy
- Mimi
- Tilly
- Jake
- Mrs S
- Wise Chorus 1-6 students
- Music makers

Props

- Collars × 3
- Leads × 2
- Dog poop bags

Precis

Chewy doesn't want to go to school. The thought of it makes him feel physically sick. Unsurprisingly, Mimi loves going to school.

Chewy's hair-parents offer him conflicting advice on how to deal with any bullying at school.

Mimi suggests Chewy gets help from the school counsellor, Mrs S, because managing bullying is a life skill which we all need.

Mrs S suggests Chewy try out new ways to deal with being bullied and challenges Chewy to consider what the bullies want to get out of the dynamic/relationship with the person they are bullying.

Mrs S further suggests Chewy is making himself more of a target and giving away his power, because bullies can smell distress, fear, and anger. However, bullies have the same capacity for being scared or angry as he does. This perspective surprises Chewy and gives him food for thought.

Concept: The 'ignore it' and 'fight back' approaches are outdated and proven to be ineffective

Evidence-based practice in psychology shows that well-meaning advice to manage bullying by suggesting, 'Do nothing, walk-away or tell the bully to stop' does not work.

Why?

Because unless targeted children are taught how to manage their reactions, they will betray their true feelings – fear, distress, anger. Even if targets are convinced that they 'did nothing', their anxiety is reflected in their voice, body language, and words. They may freeze, turn away or look upset, scared or angry. These reactions feed the bully's power and reinforce that their bullying has worked.

Concept: Reactions which keep the bullying game/cycle alive

The target gives away their power by revealing their stressors to the bully.

The bully can hone in on those vulnerabilities.

Bullies can sense fear, anger or distress in someone which makes that person a target. Reactions (fear or anger) to being bullied give bullies what they want i.e. the target gives away their power to the bully.

💬 Discussion prompts

Chewy doesn't want to go to school. Why not?

What advice do Chewy's hair-parents give him to cope with being bullied?

Have you ever been given similar advice? What were you told?

Did you try to implement that advice? If so, how did it work for you?

Mrs S explains that such advice, while well intentioned, is not effective. Instead, she asks Chewy to consider things from a different perspective; to try something different. She asks him to consider the question: 'When you get bullied, how do the bullies want you to react?'

Were you surprised to hear her ask that question? Why?

Mrs S goes even further and asks Chewy why he wants to 'give the bullies want they want?' and tells him he's giving away his power. Do you agree with her?

Have you ever felt you were giving away your power when you were bullied?

Or if you haven't experienced being bullied directly, when you've witnessed someone being bullied, can you relate to the idea they are giving away their power? How would that feel?

Concept: Stressors; everyone has them

Those factors/sensitivities which can make us vulnerable and reactive.

A 'stressor' is something that causes you to feel stressed or tense or anxious. It can be a situation, or a person and how they behave or something about yourself you don't like. We all have them and at certain times in life they are worse than other times.

What's interesting is that a stressor to one person may be completely neutral to another.

Or perhaps that factor helps one person achieve their goals, whilst for another person that same factor proves very stressful.

We are all different and influenced by our backgrounds, our personalities and our experiences.

Activity: Identify your stressors

Using Worksheet B, write down the stressors in your life.

Identifying my stressors

Write down the stressors in your life under the headings in the first column. In the second column, write down how the stressor makes you feel. There are no wrong or right answers and you do not have to fill in the columns if they don't relate to you.

Your answers are private – you do not have to share them unless you choose to.

Stressor	How I feel
My physical abilities	
My schoolwork (academic abilities)	
At school with my friends	
At school with other students who are not my friends	
At school with my teacher	
At home with my family	
My appearance	
Other	

Concept: Our backgrounds can influence our stressors

Families come in different structures and sizes.

They range from traditional families with a mum and a dad to LGBTQI parents, re-partnered parents and step-siblings to single parent households and everything in between.

It's interesting to compare and think about the differences and how they may affect us.

You first learn how to respond to the world through your family and their interactions.

You learn empathy, compassion and how to manage conflict.

You may have learned these things in a way which is helpful to you or perhaps you have learned ways which do not serve you well when you interact with your peers at school.

Remember that there is no such thing as either a 'normal' family or an 'ideal' family. Indeed, what to the outside world might look like ideal, could be a very different reality behind closed doors.

Activity: What family is that?

Please emphasise this is not an exercise in making judgments about differences in family types. Rather it is about recognising the range of ways families can be formed in society today.

In small groups discuss:

- What type of family do you come from?
- Who are its members? (some may be step-family who might come and go, extended family who may or may not live with you, and don't forget about pets and their special role in your families)
- How often do you get together?
- How many kids in your group/class come from a family similar or different to yours?
- In what ways does your family influence your social skills?

- For example, how do you socialise when you all get-together?
- What social skills get modelled by the adults in your family?

Debrief the group discussions as a class and any insights you've discovered.

Concept: Bullies are human beings too

Bullying is actually about behaviour. It should not define the whole person.

A person may exhibit bullying behaviours in one setting but not in others.

Indeed, the person who is a 'bully' is one situation, might be a 'bystander' in another or even a target!

It's important to remember that we are all human beings with the full range of emotions and vulnerabilities. Everyone experiences fear and anger at times.

Remember each and every one of us can feel the full range of emotions even if we 'act tough'.

Discussion prompts

Do you agree that someone can be a bully in one situation and a target in another?

Have you ever witnessed that?

Consider the situation where a kid who is a bully at school (even a really awful, terrifying bully) goes home every day to be cruelly bullied by a sibling or a parent.

Does thinking about the situation where that same kid suffers from being a target at home make you look/think/feel about them differently?

How?

Activity: Emotional mirroring

Divide into pairs.

Take turns to act out/mirror emotions using a range of expressions and body language.

One person starts and the other has to reflect back (mirror) exactly what they see.

Do this in silence but express yourselves in as many ways as you can.

Now swap roles.

Activity: What dog am I?

In Scenes One and Two we meet a number of characters with very different personalities.

Ask yourself to imagine: *'If I were a dog, which breed would I be?'*

Step 1

Think about which breed you most relate to, which most aligns with your personality.

Research the physical and personality characteristics of various dog breeds until you find the right fit for you. You might decide you are a mix of breeds.

Note down the key characteristics of your breed especially the behavioural aspects.

And give yourself a name!

Step 2

In character as your dog, introduce yourself to the class including:

- your breed
- some characteristics you've learned about 'yourself'
- your chosen name.

Step 3

After that round of introductions, as a class discuss:

- Did one or more dog characters seem more dominant than the others?
- Did one or more dog characters seem more cautious?
- Were any of the dog characters intimidating?
- Were the differences in the dog characters obvious?
- How do you feel about aspects of your dog character that you feel are different to others?
- What are the challenges of being different to the main group?
- What are the benefits of being different?

SCENE THREE

Cast

- Mrs S
- Chewy
- Diesel
- Mellow

Props

- Collars × 4

Precis

Mrs S wants Chewy to take advice from Diesel because Chewy is unintentionally feeding the bullying cycle by reacting just as the bullies want him to – i.e. by being angry, scared or sad.

Diesel advises that Chewy needs to learn to identify and manage his feelings so he becomes less frightened of them.

Mellow offers his advice on how he manages his fears. He recommends a physical approach. By adopting strong, confident body language it helps him feel more confident.

Concept: There are four main categories of feelings

The four main types of feelings are: glad, sad, mad and bad.

By identifying their feelings, students learn to understand them and in turn, can learn to manage their reactions. Importantly, they can learn to change their reactions when they are bullied so the cycle of bullying is stopped.

⟨≡⟩ Discussion prompts

Diesel tells Chewy he needs to get in touch with his inner mammal.

What do you think he means?

Why is it important?

Activity: Name the feelings

Diesel teaches Chewy that there are four main categories of feelings – mad, glad, sad and bad – and that the first step in learning to manage them is to learn how to identify them.

Brainstorm as a class all the words or phrases you can think of which describe the four main feelings. Write them up on a whiteboard. Examples are included below for teachers to assist with brainstorming.

GLAD aka HAPPY	SAD aka DOWN
Excited	Depressed
Pleased	Gloomy
Elated	Miserable
Ecstatic	Dismal
Peaceful	Sorrowful
Joyful	Dejected
Jolly	Unhappy
Satisfied	Moody
	Shitty

MAD aka ANGRY	BAD aka SCARED
Annoyed	Fearful
Furious	Anxious
Aggravated	Confused
Frustrated	Stressed
Irritated	Nervous
Exasperated	Worried
Cross	Tense
Livid	Frightened
	Afraid
	Terrified

Activity: Identify your feelings

Think of the various feelings in different situations you've experienced over the past week.

Write them down, placing them in the appropriate category on Worksheet C.

Some examples:

- MAD – I got very annoyed when my mother told me to get off my device even though my friends were allowed to keep 'chatting' on theirs.
- GLAD – I was really pleased with the mark I received for an assignment.
- BAD – I didn't empty the dishwasher even though it was my turn and then my father had to do it and it made him late for work.
- SAD – I heard my parents arguing about money and then I felt stressed all day.

If you had really strong feelings/emotions, they might fit into two or more categories.

Identify your feelings

Think of the different feelings you've experienced over the past week.

Write them down in the relevant category – describing the situation and the feeling it produced in you.

MAD aka angry	GLAD aka happy
SAD aka down	BAD aka scared

💬 Discussion prompts

When you did the last activity, were there any feelings you didn't know how to categorise?

Sometimes it's hard for us to analyse our emotions and reactions. Why do you think it's hard?

Even if it's difficult or challenging, it's helpful to keep trying to understand our feelings so we can better understand ourselves.

Do you agree?

Why or why not?

Activity: Try on an emotion

Everyone stands up. The teacher calls out an emotion one at a time. As an emotion or feeling is called out each student explores the emotion by acting it out, in their own way, using their body.

- Anxiety
- Fear
- Sorrow
- Cowardice
- Intimidation – being intimidating
- Intimidation – feeling intimidated
- Fury
- Happiness
- Confidence
- Shame
- Embarrassment

Activity: Wear a feeling

Divide class into pairs. Nominate one member of the pair as A and the other as B.

Student A 'wears a feeling' – acts it out without using words.

Student B guesses what they're feeling.

Swap roles and repeat the exercise with a new feeling. Swap and repeat several times.

Class discussion debrief:

- How easy or hard was it to show or identify feelings?
- What else can you do to interpret someone's feelings when you can't read their face?

Activity: Colour your feelings

This activity can help you get in touch with your inner mammal and help you learn to identify your feelings.

Draw a picture of yourself – head to feet.

Without thinking too hard about it, colour it in according to how you are feeling today – using the four main feelings and the following code.

- Happy – yellow
- Sad – blue
- Mad – red
- Bad – orange

For example, if you feel fear in your belly, then colour your belly area in orange.

Or if you feel mad or angry in your hands, then colour your hands in red.

Once you've finished, take a moment to reflect on the colours you gave yourself.

Do any of them surprise you?

⌈⊜ Discussion prompts

Do you think your 'inner mammal' is always the same?

Is it static or does it change depending on the situation?

Why or why not?

Activity: Dealing with feelings

As a class, brainstorm ways you can release negative feelings and enjoy positive feelings.

Happy:

- Listen to music
- Sing a song
- Dance
- Share with a friend

Sad:

- Read a sad poem or listen to sad music
- Cuddle a stuffed animal
- Pat a real animal
- Talk to a friend or trusted family member
- Write a poem about your feelings or draw your sadness

Angry:

- Do some exercise
- Scream into your pillow (helps release your angry energy but keeps it private)
- Write in a diary or journal
- Illustrate your anger
- Tell your friends or a trusted family member

Anxious:

- Deep breathing or a mindfulness technique
- Eat or drink something soothing or calming (e.g. a hot drink)
- Watch something fun and distracting on YouTube
- Talk to a friend or a trusted family member

Concept: Eye contact is important in most parts of Australian culture but there are some exceptions

The eyes have a universal language. Humans process information from the gaze of others to understand them and maintain social relationships. However, what is being communicated can vary from culture to culture.

💬 Discussion prompts

Diesel says he usually looks other dogs in the eye but he knows that some breeds avoid eye contact. If that's the case, he respects that and adjusts his behaviour accordingly.

Do you come from a family where eye contact is considered rude?

Have you ever met people for whom it is impolite? How did you handle the situation?

Activity: Cultural advisor brief

Pretend you are working in the Australian government's cultural advisory department.

There is a conference about to start with representatives from the following:

- Japan
- Korea
- United States
- China
- Turkey
- United Kingdom
- France

The Minister of Culture is worried about being 'culturally sensitive' to the delegates and has urgently requested a report on:

- which cultures prefer eye contact and what it means
- which cultures avoid eye contact and why it can be considered rude or threatening
- any additional information you come across which may be useful to the Minister

Divide into small groups and allocate one culture to each group.

Research your allocated culture and its norms around eye contact and prepare a written report for the Minister.

Present a short verbal briefing of your findings.

💬 Discussion prompts

You are asked to give a welcome to country address to a First Nations group of elders visiting your school. Should you make direct eye contact with the elders?

Does your answer differ depending on which part of the country the elders come from?

How would you find out this important information?

Activity: Charting global differences in communication

Research the following examples of body and facial language and how they differ from culture to culture:

- Showing soles of feet
- Hands in pockets
- Slouching
- Bowing
- Sitting with legs crossed
- Pointing
- Animated expression
- Smiling
- Handshakes

Make an illustrated chart showing the differences.

Concept: The value of being 'discerning'

Discernment enables a student to assess situations, pay attention to various clues, approach decision making thoughtfully and ultimately choose well according to their needs, values and life situation.

By learning to use their judgment and common sense, they can work out who is *worth* being their friend.

Discussion prompts

Hammer advises Chewy to be discerning about who he chooses to hang out with and explains that 'discerning' means 'having or using good judgment'.

Can you think of a situation where being discerning is critical to your physical survival?

What are some examples?

What about a situation where it is important to your social survival?

Activity: Word detecting

In pairs, brainstorm and research a list of synonyms for 'discerning'. If you find an interesting synonym which you don't understand, write down the word and its definition to share with the class.

Make a master list as a class.

Activity: Use your judgment

Write down three situations in which being discerning is very important to you personally.

🗨️ Discussion prompts

Mellow said to Chewy that part of being discerning was working out which dogs were 'nice to most but mean to some' and steering clear of them.

Have you ever noticed that some people are friendly to some types of people or groups but mean to others?

Do you have any examples you're comfortable sharing?

How does it make you feel when a friend of yours is being mean to another person or group?

Do you feel pressure to join them in being mean?

Do you ever challenge them about the mean behaviour?

Concept: Your body can help your brain

If a target is being bullied and feeling anxious, they'll show this in their body movements.

Frequently it will show up as jiggling, wriggling or moving tentatively. Bullies can read the target's body movements and identify that they're feeling fearful.

Students can help take ownership over the way they move so that a bully cannot identify their sensitivities. They can learn to use their bodies to help their brain by taking a physical approach to building confidence.

Breathing is something we do naturally and we don't usually need to think about.

When we are relaxed and feeling the 'glad' emotions, we naturally breathe slowly and deeply. When we're feeling the bad, mad or sad emotions, we take short, sharp breaths.

We do this instinctively to enable our survival (fight, flight or freeze reaction).

Bullies, like animals, can sense our altered pattern of breathing. If they believe we'll attack, they'll attack first.

Therefore, it's for our benefit to learn how to breathe in a relaxed manner. Like all things worthwhile, it takes practice. There are many techniques and it's a matter of finding the one which works for you.

⟨⟨≡⟩ Discussion prompts

Have you ever noticed changes in your breathing when you're anxious or scared?

What are they?

What happens?

How did you manage the situation?

Activity: Breathe life into your classroom

In *The Bully Blocker,* Mellow says standing up straight helps him breathe more deeply.

That in turn leads to him feeling confident and speaking more clearly.

Divide the class into three groups and allocate each group an age appropriate breathing method. For example:

- Deep breathing
- Alternative nostril breathing
- Lion's breath

Each group researches the method and practices the technique.

Prepare a short presentation and teach the rest of the class what you have learned including a practical demonstration.

Activity: Channel some confidence

Note – this activity works well with a device where students can film each other. If this is not possible or preferrable in your classroom, the exercise can be done by getting the observing student to give their feedback verbally.

Choose a nursery rhyme or a short poem remembered from your early childhood.

It doesn't matter which one. For example: you could choose 'Hey Diddle Diddle', 'Humpty Dumpty', or *Now We Are Six* by A. A. Milne.

Part I

Divide into pairs – Student A and Student B.

Student A films Student B reciting the rhyme.

Student A filming (or observing) must not make any comments or give any feedback while filming.

Play back the short video together and discuss:

- Did you stand up straight? Or did you slouch? Or jiggle?
- Did you breathe deeply while you were reciting the nursery rhyme?
- Did you appear confident?
- What vibe were you giving off?
- What could you have done differently with your body to improve your confidence?

Swap roles and repeat the exercise.

Part II

In the same pairs, each of you must silently think of a super confident person (an actor, a singer, a sportsman, a friend) you admire. It doesn't matter who – as long as they are someone you think of as exuding confidence.

Imagine that your role model has magically inhabited your body and mind!

Repeat the filming exercise in Part I channelling the confidence and energy of your role model.

Take on the positive body language, clarity and confidence of speech that your role model would use.

Watch the second version of the filmed exercise and notice the differences.

Did you stand up straighter with a high head? Eyes focused? Shoulders back? A stronger voice?

Part III

Debrief the activity as a class:

- Did you change some of your behaviours from the first version – without being told what to do?
- By pretending to be confident, did you naturally assume confident behaviours?
- What body language vibe do you think is best to prevent becoming a target?
- What other tips do you have for giving off the best neutral vibe when you're in a situation where you might feel frightened or anxious about being bullied?

⌨ Discussion prompt

There's an expression, *'Fake it till you make it?'*

Many confident and successful people have used this technique while they are developing confidence skills.

Have you ever used the technique?

How did you apply it? Did it work for you?

Activity: Practice being empowered

We learnt from the last activity how we can help ourselves feel more confident with our bodies and speech by 'channelling the persona of a confident role model', 'acting confidently' or 'faking confidence.'

Now that you've had a bit of practice acting confidently, enjoy the following exercise.

Divide into different pairs from the previous activity and number yourselves as student 1 and student 2.

Instructions

Student 1 stands in front of Student 2 with feet planted firmly on the floor about hip width apart.

1 looks 2 in the eyes and says firmly,

> *I'm bored with your teases. Come back next week with some new ones.*

Swap roles.

Brief class discussion. How did it feel delivering that line with confidence?

How did it feel to be on the receiving end of that line?

Concept: The value of a neutral face and neutral posture in blocking bullies

A neutral face can be a powerful tool in blocking bullies. When we don't want a bully to know how we feel inside (distressed, fearful, angry), it's useful to put on a blank or neutral face. A neutral face makes it hard for kids being mean to react or retaliate as it blocks further engagement.

By adopting a trance-like, spaced-out or deadpan expression you're giving bullies nothing to work with.

Remember you can save your animated face, where you express your feelings, for when you feel safe. Perhaps that's with family and friends.

Similarly adopting a neutral posture is useful in blocking bullies – as opposed to slouching, jiggling, poor posture – which gives away your inner feelings.

Activity: Neutralise yourself

As Mellow taught Chewy in *The Bully Blocker*, using a neutral face can be a powerful tool in your bully blocking tool kit.

Practice your neutral face.

It can help by practicing in a mirror or filming yourself to observe your progress.

It might help to channel a security guard or a robot.

Or think of a phrase which gets you in a neutral mood.

For example, 'I'm a well-fed cat lying in the sun' or 'I'm a bored security guard.'

Now practice 'blanking your bully' in pairs. One person blanks while the other observes.

Give each other feedback on how to improve your neutral faces.

Discussion prompts

What phrase helps you get the vibe when you practice your neutral face?

Is there an image which you focus on? What is it?

Concept: A square smile is a false smile and can be exceptionally useful in blocking bullies

Fake or false smiles can be useful if you need to block connections.

You can put on a bland, square sort of smile to block bullies.

Both the top and bottom rows of teeth are slightly bared. It's like a barbed wire fence on your face. It says to others 'No matter how hard you try you're not getting through'.

Activity: Squaring off to bullies

Practice your square smile.

Form this false smile by stretching your mouth into a square shape and revealing your teeth – both top and bottom rows.

Your eyes will not be 'smiling' either. They will look vacant, absent, unfeeling.

Activity: Who's the GOAT at blanking bullies?

Divide into small groups of five to six.

Show each other your best neutral face including your square smile.

Decide who's the best in your group and nominate that person to represent your group.

Each group representative then stands at the front of the class.

The rest of the class calls out bullying statements and the representatives have to respond with neutral faces and square smiles.

Do this for a minute or two.

Then the class votes as a whole on who's the GOAT of blanking bullies.

Give the winner a round of applause!

SCENE FOUR

Cast

- Chewy
- Mimi
- Hammer
- Sunny
- Mango
- Petal
- Mrs S
- Wise Chorus 1-6
- Music makers

Props

- Collars × 7

Precis

Chewy is verbally attacked by Petal and Hammer. Chewy gets very upset but then suddenly reacts aggressively. He also barks fiercely at Sunny and Mango who are confused by his attack when they've been nothing but friendly to him.

Eventually Chewy finds himself alone and very miserable and confides in Mrs S that he's messed up again and feels lonely.

She encourages him to see that it's never easy to learn new skills and different ways of reacting. It takes time and practice and Mr S urges Chewy to work on building his confidence.

⟨≡⟩ Discussion prompts

Petal and Hammer tease and taunt Chewy a great deal in this scene.

Why did Chewy behave the way he did?

Does anyone have an example of a recent or memorable bullying incident they witnessed or were involved in? (Please change the names of the people involved to protect everyone's privacy.)

- How did the bully, target and bystanders behave in the situation?
- Discuss possible reasons why each participant (the bully, the target, bystanders) behaved the way they did.

In the last scene Mellow said that part of being discerning was working out which dogs were 'nice to most but mean to some' and steering clear of them.

Discuss how some people are friendly to some types or groups of people but then mean to others especially:

- How does it make you feel when a friend of yours is being mean to another person or group?
- Do you feel pressure to join them in being mean?
- Do you ever challenge them about the mean behaviour?

Have you ever been teased about where you came from? (a different type of family, a different suburb to your classmates, a different cultural background?)

- Have you ever felt lonely and sad because of these differences?
- How did you handle those difficult feelings?
- How would you like other people to make you feel more comfortable?
- How can you help other students to feel more comfortable when you notice they're feeling sad or lonely?

Activity: What goes on in a bully's mind?

Complete Worksheet D individually.

Discuss your answers as a group.

What goes on in a bully's mind?

1. Consider the following question and write your answer:

   What does a student believe when they bully someone (the target)?

   _____

   _____

   _____

   _____

2. Tick which of the following you think is going through the bully's mind:

   ☐ Bullying is just a game, get over it.
   ☐ It helps me become popular.
   ☐ Everyone else does it so why shouldn't I?
   ☐ The target is annoying, and they deserve it.
   ☐ The target doesn't complain, so it mustn't bother them.
   ☐ I can get away with it.
   ☐ Nobody gets hurt. It's harmless.
   ☐ Other kids do nothing so it's obviously no big deal.
   ☐ Nobody reports me (to the teacher or online).
   ☐ Targets don't listen to my taunts anyway so it doesn't matter.
   ☐ I won't feel any guilt when I'm older, so I don't care.

3. Write down any other thoughts which you think might be going through the bully's mind.

   _____

   _____

   _____

   _____

Concept: A healthy self-esteem is important

Self-esteem is how you feel about yourself. Liking yourself, believing in yourself, backing yourself, knowing what you do well. If you think unkind words about yourself, put yourself down, criticise yourself a lot– we call that low self-esteem.

Having a low self-esteem can greatly affect the relationships you have with other people.

It can also lead to you becoming a target for bullies.

Why?

Because the bully will sense how you feel about yourself (your vulnerabilities) and see you as an easy target for their taunts.

⌨ Discussion prompts

Mrs S says to Chewy:

> *One thing I know for sure is that you're not helping yourself by being a bully to yourself.*

> *We need to work on building your confidence ... and that means in here* (taps her head)

Sometimes the worst bully in our lives is ourselves.

Have you ever noticed that you have an inner dialogue with yourself that is critical?

That you put yourself down in your head? That you shame yourself?

Do you think it's ever helpful to be self-critical? How?

Do you think it's harmful if you criticise yourself too much or too often?

How do you get the balance right?

Activity: Self-reflection – your inner critic

This activity should ideally be done when there is time to complete the following activity 'Nurturing your self-esteem' so the emphasis on negative thoughts is balanced by positive ones.

Note – this exercise requires self-reflection, privacy and a respectful environment.

We all have an internal voice in our minds (sometimes called an inner monologue). We silently talk to ourselves and comment on our strengths, weaknesses, choices, behaviours, thoughts, reactions and so on.

When that internal voice is unkind, judgmental and critical rather than friendly and compassionate, it is referred to as our inner critic. We are often harder and more critical of ourselves than we are of others.

Using Worksheet E fill in your responses to the statements.

Activity: Nurturing your self-esteem

Reflect on some behaviours which have improved your self-esteem. Fill in Worksheet F.

Self-reflection – your inner critic

Write your answers to the following statements. You may feel some of these do not apply to you. If they don't, leave the line blank and move on to the next statement.

Private and confidential

I'm no good at …

_____

I look awful because …

_____

I criticise myself when I can't do …

_____

Kids don't like me because I …

_____

I don't have enough friends because …

_____

I hate these parts of my face …

_____

I hate these parts of my body …

_____

I'm bad at sport because …

_____

I'm shy and don't know what to say when …

_____

Now that you've completed your responses, take a moment to reflect on how you feel.

Harsh self-criticism usually makes us feel awful. It can even feel like we've bullied ourselves. Was that your experience?

_____

_____

Did it feel all too easy and familiar to be critical of yourself?

_____

_____

Or was this unusual for you because you usually have confident and kind thoughts about yourself?

_____

_____

Many people find their inner critic is very noisy, attention-seeking and takes up a lot of mental energy.

It's interesting to reflect on what kind of relationship you want to have with your inner voice.

Perhaps it's of some comfort to know that many adults struggle with their inner critic and the tendency to put themselves down. Some people wrestle with this all their lives unless they actively work to address their internal self-criticism. Often the help of a psychologist or counsellor can assist making such a change.

A simple way to quieten your inner critic is to reflect on your achievements and small successes. Doing this regularly helps remind you of your positive attributes. Let's do this now by filling in the Worksheet F – Nurturing your self-esteem.

Nurturing your self-esteem

Write down some successes you've had that improved your self-esteem.

Private and confidential

Appreciation (e.g. Dad was delighted when I emptied the dishwasher without him nagging me to do it.)

_____

_____

_____

_____

Problem-solving (e.g. after lots of concentration and a number of attempts, I worked out a difficult maths exercise).

_____

_____

_____

_____

Practise (e.g. I can now easily shoot a hoop because I have practiced a lot).

_____

_____

_____

_____

Compassion (e.g. I helped a sad friend feel better by listening to their problem).

_____

_____

_____

_____

Praise (e.g. my older cousin told me she really loved how thoughtful I am).

_____

_____

_____

_____

Feedback (e.g. my swimming coach said my freestyle stroke has really improved since I took on board their suggestions)

_____

_____

_____

_____

Intuition (e.g. I guessed exactly what Mum wanted for her birthday – a homemade card with breakfast in bed!)

_____

_____

_____

_____

Activity: What makes a person confident?

Along with Princess Catherine and Michael Phelps, there are increasingly more people who are prepared to share the vulnerable sides of themselves.

In pairs or small groups, research successful people who openly share their own mistakes, failures and shortcomings. It might be a sports person, a musician, a scientist, a politician, an actor, an artist or an activist.

Find out what insights they have made about themselves.

What tips for building self-esteem or overcoming setbacks do they have?

What life wisdom have they gained from their experiences?

Share your findings with the class.

Activity: Interview someone you admire

Think of one or two adult people you know personally whom you admire. It might be a family member or friend or a teacher.

Interview them about how they achieved personal confidence. Ask them if they had any roadblocks or particular challenges to overcome and how they managed them.

Report back to your class – sharing their insights, and anything you have learned from the person you admire.

⌬ Discussion prompts

Mrs S says it is never easy to learn new skills and that it takes time and practice.

She recommends that Chewy be kind to himself and acknowledge the progress he has made – even though it's not perfect.

Do you think that is good advice? Why or why not?

Do you know what the word 'linear' means? In your experience, is learning a new skill a straightforward and linear process?

What is the best psychological approach to take when learning a new skill?

What techniques do you use to encourage yourself when you hit a roadblock in your learning?

SCENE FIVE

Cast

- Mrs S
- Chewy
- Ziggy
- Wise Chorus 1-6
- Music makers

Props

- Collars × 3

Precis

We learn that Ziggy used to be under a lot of stress when she was a racing dog. She was subjected to mental tactics in attempts to unnerve her before a race.

To cope she learned the art of the comeback. In other words, she learnt not to give away her power by using retorts (comebacks) to block the bullying.

Mrs S and Ziggy demonstrate how to practice comebacks.

The Wise Chorus alerts us to the critical fact that science shows that bullying can harm your brain.

Concept: Fight/flight/freeze

Like all other mammals, when we experience a situation as life-threatening, our survival instinct is triggered.

This instinct is called the 'fight/flight/freeze' reaction. Aka the 3 Fs.

- **Fight** – become aggressive
- **Flight** – run away
- **Freeze** – stay still

This instinct operates as our internal safety regulator. Our brains are very clever at protecting us.

Part of our brain (the amygdala) sends a message to another part (the hypothalamus) to take action.

Our brain sends a message to our adrenal glands (which sit like a hat above our kidneys). Then our brain releases powerful hormones to help us manage the 'fight/flight/freeze' instinct.

These stress hormones include cortisol and adrenaline. At the same time, our other bodily functions shut down.

It is important to understand this sequence of processes in our brain and body because exactly the same processes happen when we are bullied.

When we are bullied, we find it harder to breathe deeply. In turn that reduces our oxygen intake and we have less breath to neutralise our stress.

Then the brain releases the powerful hormones to help manage the 3F reaction.

When the bullying episode is over our body functioning should return to normal.

💬 Discussion prompts

As humans, like dogs, we are categorised as mammals in scientific terms.

What's the definition of a mammal?

If a mammal gets frightened, what reactions do we have?

Activity: Do you fight, flee or freeze?

Imagine the following:

> You're on a school excursion to the Northern Territory to explore the landscape and animal life. After a presentation by a guide where you learned about local reptiles and amphibians, the class is taken on a bus tour to view a remote swamp area. After travelling in the bus for over an hour, you're given a short break so everyone can stretch their legs and take photos. The guide warns you not to stray too far.
>
> Somehow you become separated from your class. You must have been absorbed in taking selfies and didn't realise you'd strayed from the group …
>
> You call out but no one answers you. How has this happened? Where's the bus?
>
> You start to panic.
>
> Where are your classmates? You cannot see or hear anyone.
>
> Suddenly you hear an explosive sound and you spin around.
>
> A huge saltwater crocodile (aka a saltie) is thrashing about in shallow water less than ten metres from you …

What do you think your response would be?

Out of the 3Fs, which one do you think you'd instinctively do?

Would you run for your life, stay and fight it out with the croc or freeze like a statue and hope it gets bored with the look of you and slithers away?

While some responses may be better suited to certain situations, like facing down a croc, we all respond differently when afraid. Regardless of your default response, you can learn to control your emotions and thus your reactions when confronted with a bully.

Draw a cartoon of yourself being terrified by a 'saltie' and your likely response and reactions (both physical and verbal).

Activity: Teaching your peers

You've been asked to deliver a short lesson on the survival instinct to the kids from your class who were absent on the day you studied it.

Work in small groups of 4-6 students to research and prepare the lesson.

Once you've prepared and practiced the lesson together, present it to the rest of your class.

Concept: The brain is a complex organ

Amongst other parts, the brain has:

Neurons

Our brains have an extensive neural network (made up of neurons).

Neurons are a type of cell (a nerve cell) that send messages from your body to the brain and back to the body. The messages allow you to do everything from breathing to talking, eating, walking, and thinking.

Hormones

Substances called hormones are extremely important and influence everything we do from eating and walking to feeling, thinking and behaving.

A hormone is a chemical substance that acts like a messenger in the body.

After being made in one part of the body, hormones travel to other parts of the body where they help control how cells and organs do their work.

For example, you may have heard that insulin is a hormone made in the pancreas which helps our body control its blood sugar levels.

Activity: What's a brain look like? (mid primary)

Find an image of the brain showing its main parts. Identify where the amygdala and the hypothalamus are located.

Research the function of both the amygdala and the hypothalamus.

Write a short report.

Activity: What's a brain for anyway? (upper primary onwards)

You have been commissioned as a freelance writer and artist for a leading scientific magazine. They need an image and short report which illustrates how the brain functions, including the role of the amygdala and the hypothalamus.

Work in pairs or small groups to fulfil the brief.

Choose a format and style which suits your artistic flair.

Concept: The science of how the brain can be harmed by bullying

What's the connection between neurons and hormones with bullying?

When we hurt ourselves physically (for example, when we fall over and scrape our knee or hit our head) it hurts and we feel *physical pain*. When this happens, our brain fires up to acknowledge the pain. What's fascinating is that the same region in the brain will fire up when we experience a *non-physical pain* (social pains like being bullied, humiliated or ostracised).

Conversely if we feel a *physical pleasure* (such as eating delicious food or dancing to music we love – use other age-appropriate examples!), it lights up the same part of our brain as *non-physical (social) pleasure* (such as being respected, treated fairly or caring for others).

Why do the same parts of the brain light up regardless of whether it's physical or non-physical pain and physical or non-physical pleasure?

Scientists think it could be part of our evolutionary social survival mechanism. That is, we are designed this way to help us survive as mammals. It therefore follows that if someone is repeatedly bullied, and the part of their brain that feels physical pain is lit up again and again, it can cause damage. Eventually the brain gets changed because of these damaging messages sent to it.

The outcomes of these repeated processes

We all need a moderate amount of stress to survive and get on with life by doing our chores and homework, make arrangements and so on. BUT too much stress is extremely harmful. It's like living with an untamed lion in your home.

You never know when it's going to attack you. You never feel safe. You can never relax.

If we feel constantly under stress or attack – which is how humans feel when they've been bullied and *fear being bullied at some time in the future* – our 3F reaction remains switched on.

Our stress response system remains activated and we get overloaded with stress hormones. This leads to exhaustion, break down and burn out.

The consequences of a changed brain can:

- affect our ability to trust others.
- stunt the development of our emotional and social resilience.

In summary what the science teaches us is:

- Bullying is not a harmless activity.
- School bullying can injure a target's life forever.
- Regardless of how subtle the bullying may be, when bullying threatens our self-esteem and social belonging, it triggers our survival instinct. It catapults us into survival mode and harms our current and future wellbeing.
- Bullying can literally hurt our brain and change it.
- It must be taken seriously.

Excessive stress hormones can disrupt nearly all our bodily processes and functions. Constant stress leaves us hyper-alert and unable to repair damage in our bodies and brains.

As you can see from the science of the physical reactions which take place in our bodies, bullying can literally hurt our brain and change it.

💬 Discussion prompts

The Wise Chorus says:

Sometimes they don't appreciate
Bullying causes pain
And, if it goes on for too long
Will really harm your brain!

Does that statement make scientific sense? If so, how?

Activity: Fill in the gaps - damage or change (mid primary)

If someone is repeatedly bullied, and the part of their brain that feels physical pain is lit up again and again, it can cause _____.

Eventually the brain gets _____ because of the damaging messages sent to it.

Activity: A creative brain (extension)

Pretend you are a brain. You live in a target who is being bullied a lot at school.

Write a poem or a short story about how it feels to be that brain.

Write from the brain's perspective!

There are no rules about what should be included in your story or poem but here are some possible ideas:

- The bullying situation
- Why the target in which you live is being bullied
- How it is affecting you
- Whether or not you're worried about the bullying's effect on your health
- How you'd like to protect yourself
- What you'd like to say to the bully attacking the target in which you live
- What you'd like to change

Share your story or poem with the class if you'd like to.

Concepts: Retorts or comebacks

Let's make sure we understand what retorts in the bully blocking game are not!

You are not playing 'insult tennis' with the bully where you lob insults back and forth.

You are not slamming a bully with a taunt or tease of your own.

The aim is to block the game (shut it down) by retorting in such a way that the bully is not getting what they want and you (the target) retain or take back your power, instead of giving it away.

Activity: Permission to put on your bully hat!

In small groups write down some mean taunts or teases you have heard or received recently.

They might have been at your school, on the bus, at another school, online or on TV.

Aim for coming up with at least five of them. More if you can.

When you've finished, hand them to your teacher so they can be written on a board for everyone to see.

Discuss as a class:

- Are some teases more common than others?
- Why do they hurt?

Keep the teases on the board as they will be used again in the next activity – 'Put on your retort cap'.

Concept: What makes an effective retort

The most effective retort is the one a target is comfortable saying.

A target might only feel confident enough to start with short retorts and then make their way up to a longer reply as their confidence with bully blocking grows.

As long as the retort is assertive (and not passive or aggressive), a target is doing well and can feel proud of their efforts.

Practice is key. Writing down retorts is very helpful while building retorting skills.

Some examples of the various types of retorts

Short retorts:

- And?
- Whatever.
- Thanks for your feedback.

Longer retorts:

- You have a different way of viewing things.
- I checked my star sign for today and I knew this would happen.
- Have you thought about wording that differently?

Retorts where the target acts calm and says something neutral and non-threatening:

- Really?
- Hmm fancy that.

Retorts which challenge or diffuse mean words:

- Bully: 'Bitch.'
- Target: 'How can I be a bitch when I'm not a dog?'
- Bully: 'Dickhead.'
- Target: 'Hmm. Show me a photo of that?'

Retorts which change the subject – it can be unrelated to the tease:

- Bully: 'You smell like a dodgy public toilet.'
- Target: 'And I'm a fan of the Matildas.'

Retorts which change the tease into something constructive:

- Bully: 'Yuck you're a Muzzie.' (Muslim)
- Target: 'Along with about 25% of the world's population.'
- Bully: 'Gross, you're a Jew.'
- Target: 'Did you know that Jewish merchants introduced Chinese pasta to Italy?'

Retorts which reframe or relabel the tease into something positive:

- Bully: 'You never do anything right.'
- Target: 'I manage to keep breathing.'

Retorts which agree and acknowledge the tease:

- Bully: 'You're so pathetic.'
- Target: 'You're right.'

Retorts which thank the bully:

- Bully: 'You're hopeless at basketball.'
- Target: 'Thanks for telling me.'

Retorts which confuse:

- Bully: 'Shut your face.'
- Target: 'Why don't you put on your swimmers and practice your back stroke?'

Retorts which question or clarify:

- Bully: 'You're such a bitch.'
- Target: 'Do you have any kibble for me?'

Retorts which intellectualise:

- Bully: 'You're a dumb bum.'
- Target: 'Hmm. My brain's in my head not my bum.'

Other examples:

- Bully: 'You're such a nerd.'
- Target: 'No, I'm still in training.'

- Bully: (sarcastic) 'Oh you're so beautiful. Did you have plastic surgery?'
- Target: 'No I'm made like this. I've got amazing genes.'

- Bully: 'Get lost you jerk.'
- Target: 'No I think *you* should go. It's bad for your reputation to be seen with a nerd like me.'

Note that a target can always get in first if they know or think they will be bullied about something. By making fun of themselves the target takes away the bully's power.

For example,

- 'Hi. I'm Ollie. But my sister calls me THE WHALE.'

OR

- 'You might want to hold your nose; I have to sit next to you today.'

OR

- 'I'd like to go but we can't afford that.'

Activity: Put on your retort cap

Using the examples of mean teases and taunts the class came up with in the previous activity – *'Permission to put on your bully hat,'* work in small groups to write effective retorts to block them.

Brainstorm as many comebacks as you can.

Write a list and then share your efforts with the class.

💬 Discussion prompts

What two main strategies did Ziggy use in her racing days to stop the other dogs 'getting inside her head'?

Have you ever used retorts to block someone?

Was it easy for you?

Activity: Take two!

Divide into pairs. One student takes on the role of Ziggy and the other student plays Mrs S.

Really embrace your roles and get into character!

Re-read the section in Scene Five of *The Bully Blocker* aloud to each other, from the line:

MRS S   *Hey Ziggy you're offending my eyes. You fat slob!*

down to the line:

ZIGGY   *And my farts are just like yours.*

When you're finished swap roles and read the script aloud to each other again.

Discuss as a class:

- Which role did you prefer to play?
- Why?
- Why do you think practicing role plays from scripts is useful when you're learning to change your reactions?

SCENE SIX

Cast

- Mrs S
- Chewy
- Mimi
- Comrade
- Wise Chorus 1–6
- Music makers

Props

- Collars × 4
- An e-device – phone, tablet

Precis

Mrs S suggests to Chewy that he continue to practice his retorts at home. Using a mirror or a phone to record himself.

Mimi reveals she is being cyber bullied by Chi Chi who is spreading lies about her online.

Chewy comforts Mimi using his newly learned understanding and skills about how to manage bullying.

Comrade teaches Chewy about the art of making friends.

Concept: Cyberbullying is real and rife

Cyberbullying and cyberbullies have the following characteristics:

- Takes place over digital devices – phones, computers, tablets etc
- Includes sending, posting or sharing negative, harmful, false or nasty content about another (e.g. abusive material, online sexting, stalking, scams, death threats, harassment)
- Online bullies are often more devious than face-to-face bullies and can bully 24/7
- Invades vulnerable students' rights to equality, dignity and privacy
- Can lead to stress, breakdown and even suicide by targets
- Cyberbullying is criminal behaviour and against the law in some countries

Interesting fact

During the COVID-19 pandemic it was discovered that kids bully each other less when they are stuck at home, unable to attend school except online (Vaillancourt et al 2021).

Possibly there's no fun in bullying someone if the bully can't see the target's distress the following day at school …

Options for a target

- Don't reply – just block and report
- Or reply with 'Your message has been forwarded to the police'
- Keep a record of evidence including screenshots of abusive texts, images and give the evidence to the school and police
- Change passwords frequently
- Block the bully's email address and server
- Alter your voicemail to a generic greeting
- Seek help including from police or cyber helpline

Encourage students to be an upstander not a bystander – record and report any bullying they witness online.

⚟ Discussion prompts

What does social media mean to you? What types of social media do you use?

Is it an opportunity to connect and communicate with others? Get information?

Is it a positive or negative experience for you?

Discuss a situation where you, or your family, had a negative experience.

How did it make you feel?

Are there some types of social media you are not allowed to access?

Are your parents strict about the time you spend on social media?

Are there some types they prevent you from using?

If so, why do you think they give you boundaries for your use of social media?

What are the main ways students are bullied online?

How does it affect students, now and later on?

Why do people make comments online that they would be too afraid or uncomfortable making if the target was standing in front of them?

What can you do if you witness cyber bullying?

What can everyone do to stop cyber bullying?

Activity: What do you think was said?

In *The Bully Blocker*, we learn that Chi Chi made fun of Mimi's flea problem. But we didn't get to read what Chi Chi had written online. Your task is to channel Chi Chi, use your imagination, and write some taunting, mean lines. Or construct a post for a Tiktok clip.

This activity has two parts:

1. Choose which type of social media Chi Chi is using (Insta, TikTok, Meta, etc.) and compose some lines where she bullies Mimi. Be inventive!
2. Write Mimi's responses to Chi Chi where instead of getting upset and distressed, she posts some awesome retorts to Chi Chi and shuts down the bullying game.

Concept: The art of making friends

The art of making friends and the power of being an 'influencer' is not a new phenomenon. A book titled *How to Make Friends and Influence People* by Dale Carnegie is one of the best-selling books *and* one of the most influential non-fiction books of all time.

Fun fact – it was first published in 1936!

Friendly greeting

Your smile is the first sign of your power. You can shift your mindset from feeling powerless, hopeless and helpless towards becoming assertive and using skills to take away your bully's power.

Smiling

When you smile, a whole lot of processes happen in your brain. If it's a genuine and active smile it will make you and other people feel good.

When you use a genuine smile, people treat you differently. You are seen as more approachable, reliable and sincere.

Active smiles show respect, confidence and possible connections, maybe friendship.

Look people in the eye (unless culturally inappropriate)

Listen with a 'noddie' and show interest

If you're wanting to make friends, you can show an interest in topics that might not interest you normally.

Attentive listening (active listening) – being fully present

A communication skill which involves going beyond simply hearing the words someone else speaks.

Techniques include:

- Being fully present and attentive
- Show interest by using good eye contact
- Noticing and using non-verbal clues (noddies)
- Paraphrasing and reflecting back what you have heard
- Asking open-ended questions to encourage further responses e.g. Why? How?
- Withholding judgment and advice

Share information

By showing interest it helps build connections.

The more information you share with others without using or abusing them, the more likely they are to become friendly. However, only share personal and private information about yourself when you feel safe and comfortable doing so.

Connecting statements

Sometimes it's hard to know what to say even when you want to be involved in a conversation. By using joiners or connecting statements you can join in.

There will be slang words or lingo that are used in certain age groups.

Activity: Show us your smile

1. Demonstrate each type of smile – genuine and fake (square smile).
2. Name three people you smiled at today.
3. Make a commitment to give a genuine, friendly smile at two new people every day at school. Make sure your smile reaches your eyes!
4. Reflect on whether any of the above has made a difference to socialising at school.

Activity: Making connections

Connecting statements can be very helpful in maintaining connections when you're having a conversation.

You and your parents might use some of the following:

- Awesome
- Cool
- Wow
- Yeah
- Well done
- Sounds interesting
- And then what happened ...?

The type of joiners you use at school are probably different to those your teacher or your parents use.

Write down some expressions you use which your parents do not use.

And might not even know what they mean!

Discuss them as a class.

Concept: The difference between destructive and constructive feedback

Constructive feedback can still be embarrassing but if you get out of your own way (metaphorically speaking) – then you can objectively reflect on the feedback and make adjustments to your behaviour.

You can change things from embarrassing to empowering – a great gift to give yourself.

For example, someone calls you 'an idiot.' That's destructive feedback. It's not worth taking any notice of.

On the other hand, constructive feedback might be when your teacher tells you, 'You'd be a lot better at mathematics if you did your homework and practiced the problems.'

If it's true you're not putting the work in, then you may feel embarrassed at being caught out. Perhaps you feel embarrassed because you know you've been a bit lazy with homework the past few months. Constructive feedback helps us get better.

💬 Discussion prompts

What's an example of constructive feedback?

What's an example of destructive feedback?

Sometimes even constructive feedback can feel embarrassing or upsetting initially.

What techniques can you use to help yourself take constructive feedback onboard?

Activity: Self-reflection

Write down three pieces of feedback you've received recently. It might be formal feedback (from a parent or teacher) or it might be informal feedback (e.g. The judgmental look a friend gave you when you said something mean about another student).

Activity: Getting to know you

Comrade talks about doing a 'noddie' when she is listening to someone.

It's a way of showing interest without speaking. A way of showing full attention.

Divide into pairs – choose someone you know the least.

Decide who is Student A and who is Student B.

Student A talks for two minutes about their interests or hobbies or favourite sport.

Student B must give Student A their complete attention (even if you think you'll find Student A boring). Use your noddies. Ask questions.

See how much you can learn about Student A.

Now swap and repeat the exercise.

Debrief the activity together:

- Ask each other if you felt you had the other's full attention while you were talking.
- Did you learn something new?
- Pretend you are Mrs S and coach each other. Share positive, constructive feedback on listening, showing full attention, asking questions and any helpful suggestions you have.

Concept: Building social skills

Developing a social support network is a vital part of being human. Learning the skills to do it is part of growing up and developing into adulthood.

Some students find it easier than others.

Tips for building a social network:

1. Chit chat
2. Show interest
3. Show compassion
4. Be comfortable with yourself
5. Negotiate differences
6. Real friends are committed
7. Just do it
8. Use feedback
9. Nobody's perfect
10. Collect a variety of friends

Activity: Sell us your wisdom

Work in small groups to develop a book with the title, *The Kids' Guide to Making Friends and Building a Social Network.*

Your book will include text and illustrations of some kind.

Use the handout provided as key points to cover along with any other ideas you come up with.

Maybe it will become the next bestseller!

Handout: Tips for building a social network

1. **Chit chat** – good eye contact, smiling, chatting about things which interest you and your friend. Your manner is more important than the words you say.

2. **Show interest** – the more genuine the interest you show, the more others can reciprocate.

3. **Show compassion and empathy** – try to understand what another person is experiencing and show you care by sharing both fun and/or frustrating experiences you've had (empathy). Empathy is the building block of compassion and can help create closer bonds.

4. **Be comfortable with yourself** – all people change the roles they play depending on where they are, who they're with, how they feel at that moment and what's been happening in their life. You've probably noticed you behave differently at home, school, on holidays or at a party. That's okay and normal. You can and should still be connected to your core self at all times – feel comfortable with yourself and accept yourself as you are right here and now. That's being authentic and makes it easier for other people to relate to you.

5. **Negotiate differences** – there will always be differences of opinion between people including between friends. Sometimes one person 'wins', sometimes the other 'wins' and at times they both compromise. Find friends who listen, share and resolve differences together. Avoid those who manipulate, put you down, want everything their way or try to control you.

6. **Real friends are committed** – casual friends come and go but true friends don't take each other for granted. They care about one another, keep their commitments, show interest, have reasonable expectations of the friendship and give each other space to have other friends.

7. **Just do it** – make time for friendships in real life, make plans and stick to them. Don't spend your life glued to a device.

8. **Use feedback** – feedback is a fabulous tool for everyone. Carefully consider constructive feedback you get on how you can improve yourself, especially how you relate to others.

9. **Nobody's perfect** – everyone makes mistakes and has bad days. You won't always know why someone else behaves the way they do. Aim to not judge someone else but instead try to get to know and understand their background and experiences. No friend can be perfect.

10. **Collect a variety of friends** – it's best to have a range of friends; most will be your own age but younger and older friends are great too. As are friends from a range of places. Face to face communication is very important for building social connections and the emotional rewards of friendship. (Be wary of someone who exists only on your phone or other device that you haven't met in person.)

Activity: Ironic? Who me?

In pairs, make a list of suggestions of how NOT to behave if you want to make friends.

Use your sense of humour.

Activity: Self-reflection

Come up with a list of ideas on how you could improve your social connections.

It's a private list just for you. Remember that the person who knows you best is YOU. However, if you feel you need some input on how to manage a social situation or some feedback on an aspect of yourself, you can always ask a person you trust (a teacher, a family member or a friend).

For example:

- Become friendlier with a different classmate
- Remind yourself to ask more questions in a particular situation
- Contact someone after school for a chat about homework
- Invite a different friend to spend time with you at home and ensure they feel welcome when they arrive
- Join a new club or group to increase your circle of friends

SCENE SEVEN

Cast

- Mrs S
- Chewy
- Petal
- Hammer
- Wise Chorus 1–6
- Tilly
- Jake
- Music makers

Props

- Collars × 6
- Leads × 2

Precis

Chewy is faced with a situation to test his newly acquired skills when Hammer and Petal attempt to bully him again about his ugly mouth. Chewy manages to block their bullying and gains respect.

The Wise Chorus recap the essentials of bully blocking and Chewy graduates to being a great dog.

Concept: Focus on what you can control and reprogram yourself

What you cannot control:

- another person's behaviour

What you can control:

- your own attitude and reactions
- work on becoming a better communicator
- reprogram yourself
- work on attracting friends

Discussion prompts

Can you change other people's behaviour? Why or why not?

What do you have control over?

Do you know what a paradox is?

When Evelyn worked with bullied children she discovered an amazing paradox:

When you respect yourself, protect yourself and block bullies, most kids respect you and some will become your friends.

Do you agree with this statement? Why or why not?

Recap of the key points explored in *The Bully Blocker*

1. Science shows bullying changes your brain and damages it. Therefore, managing bullies is an important life skill.

2. Learn not to show fear or worry or anger. Ensure your body language and facial expressions do not give you away!

3. A neutral face and neutral posture are handy tools (along with a square smile when you need it).

4. Use retorts to show the teases and taunts are not getting to you.

5. Reprogram yourself to change your attitude and become a better communicator.

6. Smile!

These factors help you navigate the world, block any bullies and attract friends.

Activity: The panel

Ask for a volunteer to be a journalist with the job of investigating the latest bully blocking techniques. Choose five students to sit on a panel where the journalist interviews them about their knowledge.

Activity: Self-reflection

Complete Worksheet G. This is a completely private task. There is no obligation to share your thoughts unless you want to.

Activity: Offer your support

You've noticed someone in your class is the target of bullying by another student. You feel very upset on their behalf but you feel too uncomfortable to intervene directly and challenge the bully's behaviour. Nonetheless you'd like to offer your support without drawing attention to yourself in class.

Write them an email. You might like to include tips on how to bolster their self-confidence and suggestions of how to block bullying.

Activity: Write a letter of thanks

Pretend you are Chewy at the end of the play. You're transformed and are feeling very confident about yourself and your skills in blocking bullies. Much of this has been because of the incredible support from Mrs S.

Write her a personal thank you letter highlighting the most valuable lesson you learned and what you most appreciate about her counselling.

Activity: Debrief circle

Form a class circle. One by one go around the circle stating one or two positive things you have enjoyed while studying *The Bully Blocker*. Perhaps it's a concept, a technique for bully blocking or a character in the play you particularly liked!

Self-reflection

Reflect on the questions and then write your answers below. This is a completely private task. There is no obligation to share any of your thoughts with anyone else unless you want to.

1. Have you ever been accused of being a bully – at home or at school?

   _____

2. Have you ever used bullying behaviours such as teasing, excluding, eye rolling, criticising or gossiping? If yes, which ones?

   _____

3. How did you feel about behaving in this way? Did you ever feel good about it?

   _____

4. Did it affect the other person and if so, how?

   _____

5. Did you feel anything for your target? If so, what did you feel?

   _____

6. What could you have said or done differently that would not have been construed as bullying?

   _____

7. Have you ever wanted to apologise? If so, what would you do or say?

   _____

8. How would you feel during the apology?

   _____

9. How would you feel afterwards?

   _____

10. Additional reflections on your behaviour?

    _____

EXTENSION ACTIVITIES

🗨 Discussion prompts

Bullying has been going on for at least 3000 years and possibly longer. We know this because in Greek mythology one of the Gods, *Ares*, was known as a bully AND a coward.

What's your understanding of cowardly behaviour?

Do you agree that bullies are also cowards? Why or why not?

Can you think of any examples where a bully is genuinely respected?

Or are they given status and respect out of fear?

In other words, if you don't go along with the bully, the risk is the bully may turn on you …

Activity: 'All bullies are cowards' class debate

Divide your class into two teams (Team A and Team B) for a debate.

Team A is arguing for the affirmative – that all bullies are also cowards.

Team B is arguing for the negative – that all bullies are not necessarily cowards.

Brainstorm with your team the main points of your argument.

Appoint three spokespeople to represent your team in the debate.

Hold the debate.

Alternative debate topics:

- All bullies have personal issues
- All bullies are insecure

Activity: Rewrite part of Scene Four

Revisit Scene Four where Hammer and Petal tease Chewy about his background.

Rewrite the lines in the scene from Petal's line:

PETAL   *Did you know I'm a fourth-generation pit-bull terrier? Tell me Chewy, what breed are you again?*

Rewrite it so that Chewy eventually stops the bullying game. He doesn't let the teasing get to him. Instead, he blocks the taunts about his pedigree with some clever retorts so that Hammer and Petal are finally left speechless because their bullying doesn't work.

Activity: Writing exercise

Choose your favourite scene from *The Bully Blocker.*

Write a poem or a rap song retelling the story of that scene.

PHYSICAL BULLYING AND SOCIAL EXCLUSION

There are five main types of bullying. Verbal bullying, cyberbullying and harassment or discrimination have been explored extensively in *The Bully Blocker* playscript and the resources in this book. The other two types of bullying are physical bullying and social exclusion. Both of these are briefly touched on in *The Bully Blocker*.

Physical bullying

Physical bullying includes hitting, pushing, shoving, intimidating or otherwise physically hurting another person, damaging or stealing their belongings. It also includes threats of violence. In *The Bully Blocker* the characters Diesel and Mellow empathically say:

1. Physical bullying should be reported
2. Advice to fight back is outdated
3. There are smarter ways to stop a bully

In depth exploration of how a target should react to/cope with physical bullying is deliberately not addressed in this book.

Your schools will have their own policies and procedures on managing physical bullying.

There are legal requirements (local, state and federal laws) and an ethical duty of care to uphold.

You can find Evelyn's perspective on these challenges in Chapter 12 of her book, *Bully Blocking: Empowering students to manage bullying*.

Social exclusion

Social exclusion is when the bully manipulates the group to isolate the target. It can be direct ('You can't sit with us') or indirect (with subtle, non-verbal body language). The goal is to create a group identity which becomes a powerful control mechanism. Each member knows that if they support or stand up for the target, they'll be next in line to be left out. They will become the next target. This threatening dynamic cowers group members into supporting the bully's behaviour.

Social exclusion makes a person feel unwanted and includes behaviours like cruel rumours, nasty gossip, staring, mimicking, direct exclusion, isolation and ostracism.

In *The Bully Blocker*, the character of Mimi is distressed by rumours about her flea problem. Her brother, Chewy, is subjected to being mimicked and told directly by Hammer and Petal that he is not liked or wanted.

Social exclusion is often a consequence of verbal bullying, harassment or cyber bullying as is evident in the experiences of Mimi and Chewy. There is often an overlap in the behaviours.

Evelyn's perspective on social exclusion and coping suggestions can be found in Chapters 9 and 12 of her book, *Bully Blocking: Empowering students to manage bullying*.

Discussion prompts

Are your parents aware of how your school deals with bullying?

Are they satisfied with the school's approach?

If not, do they have any suggestions?

SIGNS A STUDENT MIGHT BE A VICTIM OF BULLYING

Physical signs

- Bruises, cuts, scratches
- Stolen or damaged possessions e.g. torn clothing
- Minor aches and pains, stomach aches, headaches
- Loss of hair, skin disorders
- Under or overeating
- Unusual requests for money
- Stays close to a teacher or other adults during breaks
- Poor communication signs e.g. limited eye contact, bad posture, jiggles, mumbles
- Self-harming or threats to do so

School work signs

- School work quality deteriorates, reduced concentration, memory difficulties
- Won't participate in class activities or interact with peers in class
- Focuses solely on their studies and avoids extra-curricular activities
- Attends class irregularly and misses schoolwork

- Hides learning difficulties for fear of being ridiculed
- Hides intelligence or other talents for fear of being ridiculed
- Fears cooperative learning groups
- Avoids asking questions in class

Social signs

- Appears anxious among peers
- Sits alone in class, excluded from peers at recess and lunch time
- Regularly retreats to the library or sick bay
- Often chosen last for a team, project or game
- Poor social life

Psychological signs

- Aggressive or provocative
- Sad, miserable, depressed and teary
- More moody, irritable, snappy, sarcastic, angrier than usual
- Appears pale, anxious, distressed, withdrawn, secretive

(Adapted from *Bully Blocking: Empowering students to manage bullying* by Evelyn M. Field.)

ABOUT THE AUTHORS

Anneka Champion's early career included stints as an actor and a lawyer (BA LLB Hons University of Sydney). She is also an alumnus of NIDA in playwriting. Combining these diverse skills, Anneka worked for many years as a freelance writer in marketing and adult education, and as a facilitator in change management. Her vocation is to communicate complex ideas through simple, accessible narratives. She is especially passionate about providing children with the tools to thrive in today's complex social environment. Anneka lives in Sydney with her family which includes a much-loved whippet.

Evelyn M. Field OAM, FAPS is a psychologist, professional speaker, best-selling author and regular media commentator. She has spent more than four decades helping students and adults develop social survival skills to manage bullying in schools and the workplace. She was awarded a Medal of the Order of Australia for her initiatives in school and workplace bullying. Some of her inspiration comes from studying how animals survive socially and the recent evidence around bullying and brain trauma. As well as treating targets, she provides training for therapists, schools, organisations and participates in cruise enrichment programs. She is currently completing a book on 'Social Smarts for High-School Students.'

ACKNOWLEDGMENTS

From Anneka

I have the deepest gratitude and thanks to:

- Evelyn Field for generously sharing her impressive expertise and this project with me,
- Alicia Cohen for being an affirming, inspiring and dynamic publisher,
- Sarah Fallon for her perceptive, sensitive and measured editing, and
- Sean Doyle for his unstinting encouragement and wise counsel.

From Evelyn

A play like this evolves with the support, encouragement and inspiration of many sources. I am greatly indebted to Alicia Cohen and Sean Doyle, to Sarah Fallon and most of all Anneka who volunteered to tackle a new subject, from an author she hardly knew, to create a unique project, i.e. teaching kids how to block bullies themselves, based on the latest evidence. My hope is that her play will change how bullying is viewed, and that more students develop the life survival skills to block bullying themselves and reduce the life-long injuries that bullying causes.

Milton Keynes UK
Ingram Content Group UK Ltd.
UKHW022111251124
451529UK00010B/458